Würzburg

Portrait einer Stadt
Portrait of a Town
Portrait d'une ville

elmar hahn verlag

Würz

Fotografie: Elmar Hahn
Text: Werner Dettelbacher
Gestaltung: Klaus Schinagl

burg

Portrait einer Stadt

Impressum:

Idee und Konzeption: Elmar Hahn, Klaus Schinagl
Fotografie: Elmar Hahn, Veitshöchheim
Mit Ausnahme von Seite 8, 19, 23, 26, 31 und 101:
Klaus Bauer, Elmar Hahn Studios
Texte: Werner Dettelbacher, Würzburg
Übertragung ins Englische/English Translation:
Tina Neil, Würzburg
Übertragung ins Französische/Traduction et adaptation:
Claire Pascal, Würzburg/Paris
Textbearbeitung: Horst Büttner, Würzburg
Gestaltung: Schinagl-Design, Veitshöchheim
Litho: Offsetreproduktion Held, Würzburg
Gesamtherstellung:
Grafischer Betrieb Bonitas-Bauer, Würzburg

Printed in Germany – Imprimé en Allemagne

ISBN 3-9802214-1-5

„Würzburg ist fröhlich.
Es gehört zu jenen Städten, deren bloßer Name
die Vorstellung strahlender Heiterkeit erweckt
und das Herz rascher schlagen läßt.
Je heißer der Tag, je leuchtender die Sonne,
je blauer der Himmel,
je stärker die Kontraste von Licht und Schatten,
desto feiner wird der farbige Eindruck.“

Josef Hofmiller

FOTO
WÖHRL

Würzburg
Metropole am Main

Abenddämmerung senkt sich auf Mainlauf und Alte Mainbrücke. Maria mit dem Sternenkranz, Kilian rechts und Totnan zur Linken halten nächtliche Zwiesprache mit König Pippin, Carl Borromäus und Nepomuk, dem Brückenheiligen.

The setting sun along the Main and the Alte Mainbrücke (Old Bridge). Mary with her celestial crown, Kilian and Totnan to the left conversing with Pippin, Carl Borromäus and Nepomuk, the Bridge's saints.

Le crépuscule descend sur le fleuve et le Vieux Pont sur le Main (Alte Mainbrücke). La Vierge Marie avec son auréole étoilée, Kilian et Totnan à sa gauche, s'entretiennent avec le roi Pépin, Charles Borromée et Népomucène, le saint patron des ponts.

In Würzburg reden die Steine

Nicht nur große Sehenswürdigkeiten von europäischem Rang sprechen zu uns und vergegenwärtigen Herrschaft und Prachtentfaltung, Frömmigkeit und Todesfurcht, auch schmale Gassen und kleine Plätze, Kapellen und Kreuzgänge erzählen Episoden aus einer alten Stadt.

Mehrfach an den Rand der Vernichtung gedrängt, besonders in der fürchterlichen Brandnacht von 1945, hat Würzburg die Zeit überdauert und sprüht von pulsierendem Leben.

Wer nachdenklich durch die Stadt geht, wird an große und schwere Zeiten erinnert. An Reichs- und Hoftage der Salier und Hohenstaufen, die prachtvolle Hochzeit Kaiser Friedrich Barbarossas, aber auch an König Wenzel, der sein Versprechen brach, Würzburg zur Reichsstadt zu erheben. Er meint die Anführer der Bauern zu hören, die im „Stachel" heftig diskutieren und den verhängnisvollen Sturm auf den Marienberg beschließen. Dann lauscht er dem Te Deum nach der Universitätsgründung in der Vituskapelle der Franziskaner und vernimmt das Flehen um Schonung, als die Schweden plündern. Jubelrufe der Bürger glaubt er vernehmen zu können, als aus der von Balthasar Neumann gebauten Wasserleitung das erste Wasser floß und Hochrufe, als der erste Personenzug eintraf und die Stadt mit der großen Welt verband. Wenn er dann wieder mit wachen Augen die Neuzeit aufnimmt, kann er, auch abseits von Touristenrouten, erfahren, was einmalig ist an dieser Stadt.

Es begann mit einem Mord

Kilian, der irische Wanderbischof, und seine Gefährten Kolonat und Totnan erreichten 686 n. Chr. eine kleine fränkische Siedlung im Maindreieck.

Dort, in Virteburh, wo der Main seinen schönsten Bogen zieht, predigten und missionierten sie unter Fischern, Schiffern und Bootsbauern des Mainviertels unterhalb der Burg. Sie vergaßen auch nicht Schmiede, Wagner und Pferdeknechte auf der gegenüberliegenden Mainseite am Amtshof. Der stand auf stets hochwasserfreien Stufen, die einmal später zum Dom führen sollten.

Ganz Glaubenseiferer, zeigte Kilian keinen Sinn für laues Christentum und Rückversicherer, die zwar schon christlich waren, aber doch noch heidnische Götter und Bräuche duldeten. Kompromißlos forderte er öffentlich die Auflösung der Ehe des inzwischen getauften Amtsherzogs Gosbert. Er hatte nach heidnischem Recht die Witwe seines Bruders geheiratet. Eine Trennung hätte aber für Gailana den Ausschluß aus der herrschenden Schicht bedeutet. Aus Furcht davor ließ sie, in Abwesenheit ihres Gemahls, die Glaubensboten ermorden und unter einem Pferdestall verscharren.

752 erst fand man die Gebeine der Märtyrer unter dem Roßstall, aufmerksam gemacht durch unermüdlich scharrende Pferde. Die Reliquien wurden von Bischof Burkard zunächst in die 706 n. Chr. erbaute Marienkirche auf der Burg gebracht. In einer feierlichen Prozession überführte sie sein Nachfolger drei Jahre später über den Main in den „Salvatordom", dessen Bau bereits begonnen hatte.

Karl der Große (768-814) förderte die Verehrung des Heiligen in seinem Reich besonders und besuchte selbst in zwei großen Prozessionen (788 und 793) die Grabstätte.

Bald entdeckten Wallfahrer, daß das Wasser des nahen Brunnens gegen Augenleiden half, zumindest Augen- und Kopfschmerzen linderte. Da nicht alle herandrängenden Gläubigen in der Krypta Platz hatten, wurden die kostbar gefaßten Schädeldecken der Märtyrer mit anderen Reliquien zusammen als Heiligtümer auf den Stufen des Doms zur Schau gestellt.

Vom Hochamt zur Kiliani-Messe

Die Pilger, die von weither zum Hochamt gekommen waren, mußten essen und trinken, wollten Kerzen aufstecken und einkaufen, was es in ihren entlegenen Dörfern nicht gab. Da im August die Landbevölkerung noch mit der Ernte beschäftigt war, wurde die genehmigte Verkaufsmesse mit Jahrmarkt kurzerhand vom 17. August auf die Kilianioktav (die 8 Tage währende Kiliani-Feier um den 8. Juli) vorverlegt.

Von den „Greden", den Domstufen, die Domstraße hinunter zur Alten Mainbrücke dehnte sich die Messe, standen die Buden dicht an dicht, bis zu den Garküchnern vor dem Grafeneckart, zur Freude der Hausbesitzer, die Gewölbe und Stellplätze teuer vermieteten.

Und dann ins Vergnügen

Wo sich so viele Menschen trafen, denen das Geld locker saß, da stellten sich Gaukler und Seiltänzer ein, Akrobaten und Bärenführer, die um Brot und Käse und etliche Kupfermünzen ihre Künste zeigten, fahrendes Volk, das als ehrlos galt, kein Haus erwerben und kein Handwerk erlernen konnte. Die Obrigkeit sah den Artisten, Zahnreißern und Wunderdoktoren, auch einem Doktor Faustus, sehr auf die Finger; allein Bischof Rudolf von Scherenberg erließ 13 Meßordnungen, die sich besonders gegen Bettler und Handelsjuden wandten.

In den Jahrhunderten wechselten die Attraktionen, das Volksfest, die „Kiliani-Messe" wurde auf den Sanderrasen, dann an den Mainkai und schließlich zur Talavera abgedrängt, doch blieb die Lust am Absonderlichen und Prickelnden, an Abenteuer und Maskerade. Moritatensänger und Panoramen nahmen Kriminalroman und Fernsehen vorweg, Schießbuden und Flohzirkus, Karussell und Geisterbahn sind bis heute geblieben.

Sammelplatz aller Besucher ist das große Bierzelt, in dem Trachtenkapellen aufspielen und der Oberbürgermeister das erste Faß Festbier anzapft.

Wenn dann, am ersten Sonntagabend im Juli, die Stadt und am dritten Montagabend die Schausteller ihr Feuerwerk zünden, wenn Raketen in den Nachthimmel zischen und sich dort leuchtend entfalten, ist das Vergnügen auf dem Höhepunkt.

Wein- und andere Feste

Es begann damit, daß sich das Ritterstift St. Burkard das Vorrecht verschafft hatte, im „Hof zum Rückermain", an den ersten drei Tagen der Kiliansoktav Wein an jedermann zum halben Preis abgeben zu dürfen. Dabei legten die Stiftsherren nicht drauf, da ihr Festwein von allen Abgaben befreit war, sehr zum Verdruß der Weinwirte, deren Gäste in die Karmelitenstraße abwanderten.

Nach dem 1. Weltkrieg richtete man im alten Bahnhof (später auf dem Viehmarktplatz) ein Weinfest aus, das, zu Michaeli (29. September) beginnend, die Fässer vor der Weinlese leeren half, den Besuchern Geselligkeit und heiteren Sinn versprach. Seit 1987 wird ein Weindorf auf dem Marktplatz aufgeschlagen, wo man in einer Vielzahl kleiner Häuschen Weine aller Lagen und viele verschiedene Zuspeisen probieren kann. Da Einheimische wie Besucher auch im Juni fröhliche Geselligkeit nicht entbehren wollen, bietet das Bürgerspital ein Weinfest im malerischen Hof an, die Woche darauf kredenzt das Staatsweingut seine Schoppen im Hofgarten der Residenz. Daß da ein Bierfest der unterfränkischen Brauereien kommen mußte, war abzusehen; im Mai 1988 konnte man erstmals deren helle und dunkle Spezialitäten testen.

Das Lusamgärtchen

Im Mai 1883 wurden die alten Häuser zwischen der Martinsgasse und dem Kürschnerhof nördlich Neumünster abgebrochen und ein großer Keller für das Kaufhaus des Salomon Rosenthal ausgeschachtet. Dabei fand man die nördliche Arkadenreihe des Kreuzgangs von Neumünster, dessen Entstehung mal ins erste Drittel des 13. Jahrhunderts, mal in die Jahre 1170/80 gesetzt wird. Nachdem die Fragmente einige Zeit gelagert hatten, bot 1908 Geheimrat Bode dem Besitzer 75 000 Mark, um dieses „kostbare Denkmal staufischer Architektur und Plastik" für das Kaiser-Friedrich-Museum in Berlin zu erwerben. Von Würzburger Bürgern alarmiert, konnte Prinzregent Luitpold den Abtransport verhindern. Die Anzahlung wurde erstattet und der Kreuzgangflügel 1912 im Garten des Luitpoldmuseums der Stadt Würzburg aufgestellt.

Nach der Zerstörung des Museums 1945 plazierte man ihn an den Südrand des Lusamgärtchens. Einst wandelten hier die Stiftsherrn und lasen ihr Brevier. Fiel ihr Blick auf die Reliefs der Pfeiler, so sahen sie den thronenden Christus mit dem Evangelienbuch und St. Kilian, schauten sie zu Boden, erblickten sie die Grabsteine ihrer Vorgänger.

Herr Walther von der Vogelweide
im warmen Winternest

Daß Herr Walther im „Grashof" bei Neumünster, dem späteren Lusamgärtchen begraben liegt, erfährt man aus Notizen in den Hausbüchern des bischöflichen Kanzleivorstandes Michael de Leone. Da er als Scholaster (Schulrektor) von Neumünster die ausgezeichnete Bibliothek des Stiftes nutzen konnte, ließ er auch die Liebeslieder Walthers abschreiben. Hier erhielt Walther von der Vogelweide von Kaiser Friedrich II. ein Lehen aus dem Besitz des Stiftes Neumünster als Altersversorgung. Es war ein Vorrecht des deutschen Königs, ein erstes freiwerdendes Lehen für einen seiner Getreuen zu erbitten. So jubelt denn auch der Beschenkte :„Ich hab' mein Lehen! All die Welt, ich hab' mein Lehen, nun fürcht' ich nicht mehr den Frost an den Zehen." In Peter Rühmkorfs freierer Übersetzung fährt er fort: „Der gute König, milde König hat geruht, mich auszustatten. O meine Sommerfrische du, mein warmes Winternest!"

So begeistert kann nur jubeln, wer sein Leben lang über die Straßen zog. Walther von der Vogelweide war der größte Minnesänger deutscher Zunge, aber auch ein politischer Sänger, dessen Lieder, etwa gegen Papst und Kurie, scharf wie ein Ritterschwert waren. Zunächst stand er auf der Seite des Staufers Philipp von Schwaben, zog mit ihm von Pfalz zu Pfalz, bis er bei Bischof Wolfger von Passau Aufnahme fand. Später wechselte er auf die Seite des Welfen, des Gegenkönigs Otto IV., den er verließ, um den jungen Friedrich II., den Staufer aus Sizilien, zu begrüßen. Der verschaffte ihm, dem Fünfzigjährigen, 1219/20 eine zehn Jahre währende Pause, in der ihm die „Elegie" und das „Kreuzfahrtlied" gelangen.

Als die Stadt Würzburg ihm 1930 zum 700. mutmaßlichen Todesjahr einen Gedenkstein im Lusamgärtchen setzte, schlug man nahe den Ecken flache Näpfe ein, weil der Überlieferung nach der Minnesänger gewünscht hatte, man möge die Vögel auf seinem Grabe „weiden", also füttern und tränken. Um den Muschelkalkblock läuft als Fries der Vers Hugo von Trimbergs († 1313): „Her Walther von der Vogelweide / Swer des vergaeze der taete mir leide." Auch heute gibt es immer noch Besucher des Lusamgärtchens, die Blumen auf den Gedenkstein legen.

Vom Scheitel der Alten Mainbrücke führt die Straße geradewegs zum viertürmigen Dom. Zur Linken steht der Grafeneckart mit spitzem Helm und Sturmglocke, daneben erkennt man die Kuppel von Neumünster mit dem Zwiebelturm.

The street leads straight from the Alte Mainbrücke (Old Bridge) to the four-towered Cathedral. On the left Grafeneckart rises with its pointed rood and fire alarm; adjacent, the dome of the Neumünster and its onion tower.

Le Vieux Pont fait un dos d'âne sur le fleuve, de là on descend tout droit sur la cathédrale aux quatre tours. A gauche s'élève le Grafeneckart, tour carrée de l'Hôtel de Ville, avec son clocheton pointu, tandis que la coupole de l'église Neumünster fait, elle, le gros dos à côté de son bulbe.

Max Dauthendey – zerrissen von Fern- und Heimweh

Max Dauthendey, Sohn eines aus St. Petersburg zugezogenen Photographen, hat unter dem strengen Vater nicht wenig gelitten. Das seltsame Anziehen und Abstoßen zwischen beiden ist Hauptthema seines Werkes „Der Geist meines Vaters“. Begonnen hatte seine Wortkunst voller Sensibilität, seine farbenreichen impressionistischen Gemälde mit „Ultraviolett“, als er 26 Jahre zählte. Eines seiner Lyrikbändchen wurde in Reverenz an Walther von der Vogelweide „Lusamgärtlein“ benannt.

Mit 13 Jahren war er zum ersten Mal geflohen, kam aber nur bis Aschaffenburg. Später wird es ihn über die „Sieben Meere“ jagen, das süße Fernweh. Kaum hat er sich voller Eindrücke gesogen, da sehnt er sich nach Hause. „Hört er in Paris auf dem Markt Hähne schreien, so denkt er gleich an den Hahnenschrei auf den fränkischen Dörfern. Und in Mexiko war ihm, als läge mitten im Urwaldgetöse des Ozeans, ganz nahe, das freundliche, sonnenbeleuchtete Maintal mit den Türmen der Vaterstadt und den Weinbergen“ (Max Rößler). Auf seinen Reisen in Asien schuf er „Lingam“ (12 asiatische Novellen) und „Die acht Gesichter am Biwasee“. Diese Novellensammlung führte zur Freundschaft mit der Stadt Otsu am Biwasee, die 1979 Würzburgs Partnerstadt in Japan wurde. Obwohl seine Werke, auch der Roman „Raubmenschen“, erfolgreich waren, blieb er, ständig auf Reisen, verschuldet, mußte schließlich 1914 erneut, diesmal im Sold eines Verlages und einer Schiffahrtslinie, tief nach Ostasien hinein. Vom Weltkrieg überrascht, wurde er auf Java interniert und vier lange Jahre von Frau und Heimat getrennt. Müde vom Tropenlärm schrieb er: „Ich gehe durch die alten weihrauchblauen Kirchen Würzburgs und besuche mit Dir zusammen die Mette und die Krippenbilder des alten Käppele auf dem Nikolausberg und sehe von oben vom Platz vor der Kirche auf die Fenster unserer alten Wohnung am Main, wo die Spatzen auf den kalten Fensterbänken auf die Fütterung durch uns warten.“

Heimwehkrank starb er in Malang auf Java am 29. August 1918, 72 Tage vor dem Ende des Krieges.

Leonhard Frank – für Frieden und gegen Gewalt

Als Sohn eines Schreinergesellen 1882 im Mainviertel geboren, litt er in seiner Schulzeit unter einem tyrannischen Lehrer der Münzschule, der mit Stockschlägen und Zynismus die Klassen in panischen Schrecken versetzte. In seinem zweiten Werk „Die Ursache“, einer scharfen Anklage gegen die Todesstrafe, hat er mit ihm abgerechnet. Eine Lehre brach er ab, wurde Labordiener, Chauffeur und Anstreicher, ehe er mit einem Stipendium die Kunstakademie in München besuchen konnte. Nach Berlin übersiedelt, hungerte er sich durch und wohnte mit seiner jungen Frau Neubauten trocken. Hier überwand er die seelischen Verletzungen seiner Jugend, indem er die Sehnsüchte und Bedrückungen seiner Altersgenossen in der „Räuberbande“ (1914) in einer kargen, auf den kürzesten Ausdruck gerafften Sprache schilderte. Drei Monate arbeitete er an der ersten halben Seite, dann hatte er sich freigeschrieben. Sie endet: „Über der Stadt lag Abendsonnenschein. Ein roter Wolkenballen hing über der grauen Festung auf dem Gipfel, und im steil abfallenden königlichen Weinberg blitzten die weißen Kopftücher der Winzerinnen – die Weinernte hatte begonnen. Es roch nach Wasser, Teer und Weihrauch.“

Als der Weltkrieg ausbrach, emigrierte er als überzeugter Pazifist nach Zürich und schloß sich dem Kreis um René Schickele an. Für dessen „Weiße Blätter“ schrieb er Novellen gegen Krieg und Gewalt, die im Sammelband „Der Mensch ist gut“ 1917/18 nach Deutschland geschmuggelt wurden, voll der utopischen Hoffnung, die Menschenschlächterei könne wenigstens um einen Tag abgekürzt werden.

Noch im November 1918 kehrte er zurück. Es gelangen ihm neben Erzählungen Romane, die in Würzburg und Umgebung spielen. „Das Ochsenfurter Männerquartett“ und „Von drei Millionen Drei“ als Fortsetzungen der „Räuberbande“, dazu die Heimkehrertragödie „Karl und Anna“, die als Schauspiel und Film Aufsehen erregte. Als Hitler an die Macht kam, der Franks Bücher verbrennen ließ, floh er über die Schweiz nach Frankreich. Obwohl ausgebürgert, wurde er nach dem Kriegseintritt Frankreichs interniert, konnte gerade noch fliehen, als das Lager deutschen Truppen übergeben wurde. In Hollywood schrieb er die „Deutsche Novelle“, das Psychogramm einer Hörigkeit und in New York unter dem Schock eines Fotos des zerstörten Würzburg den Roman „Die Jünger Jesu“, der ein utopisches Nachkriegs-Würzburg zeichnete.

Nach München zurückgekehrt, gelang ihm noch der autobiographische Roman „Links wo das Herz ist“, in dem er auch seine Hoffnung auf eine gerechte sozialistische Wirtschaftsordnung niederlegte. Er starb 1961 in München.

Eine „Stätte der Freude und Bildung“

Als Bayern 1802/03 Würzburg zum ersten Mal besetzte, begann der große Ausverkauf des geistlichen Besitzes. Während der Staat die Residenz und die Weinberge der Geistlichkeit behielt, wurden die Domherrnhöfe feilgeboten, Monstranzen, Kelche und Patenen an die königliche Münze in München abgeführt, Kleinodien meistbietend versteigert.

Trotz dieser Eingriffe gab es Bürger, die sich über Erlasse der Besatzungsmacht freuten. So wurde die engherzige Zensur abgeschafft, der auch die Werke von Goethe, Wieland und Lessing zum Opfer gefallen waren. Statt der nur für wenige Tage verweilenden Theatertruppen, die erbauliche Rührstücke oder übermütige Hanswurstiaden aufführten, wurde nun dem Grafen Julius von Soden erlaubt, ein stehendes Theater zu errichten, um die Würzburger mit Opern und Schauspielen zu erfreuen und zu bilden. Trotz vieler Zugeständnisse an den Geschmack der Zeit war das private Theater 1849 am Ende. Es wurde von der Stadt übernommen, da es sich nicht mehr selbst finanzieren konnte.

Nach der Zerstörung 1945 sprangen noch einmal Bürger ein, um das Theater in der Turnhalle der Lehrerbildungsanstalt am Wittelsbacher Platz fortzuführen, bis der städtische Haushalt eine Übernahme ermöglichte.

Eine Hohe Schule der Musik

Die erste Besetzung durch Bayern war auch dem Jurastudenten Franz Joseph Fröhlich förderlich, der 1801, im Alter von 21 Jahren, eine akademische Musikgesellschaft übernommen hatte. Auf Anraten der Regierung wurde sie in ein Musikalisches Institut umgewandelt (nach Berlin das zweitälteste in Deutschland), das zunächst nur Akademikern zugänglich war, bald aber nach entsprechenden Prüfungen alle Landeskinder aufnahm.

Aus begabten Solisten stellte Fröhlich ein Orchester zusammen, das die Musikliebhaber im herrlichen Domkapitelsaal der Stadt mit alten und zeitgenössischen Komponisten bekannt machte. Unter Dr. Karl Kliebert, Direktor der Kgl. Musikschule, entbrannte ein Wettbewerb mit der „Harmonie“, einer bürgerlichen Musikgesellschaft, wer die bekanntesten Kapellmeister und Solisten nach Würzburg ziehen konnte.

Nachdem 1920 Professor Hermann Zilcher das Staatskonservatorium für Musik übernommen hatte, entwickelte er die Idee des Mozartfestes im Kaisersaal der Residenz. Solisten und Orchester dieser Hochschule für Musik sind bis heute wichtige Bestandteile bei den alljährlichen Aufführungen geblieben.

Vom Zauber der Franziskanergasse

Der Altbayer Josef Hofmiller, ein Bewunderer Würzburgs, rät uns: „Würzburg prunkt nicht nur mit den großen Sehenswürdigkeiten, die im Baedeker zwei Sterne haben, es lockt auch mit den kleinen, die es den Fremden selbst entdecken läßt, und das macht das Wandeln durch seine malerischen Gassen zu einem Genuß von seltsamen Zauber.“

Die Franziskanergasse ist eine solche Gasse voller Überraschungen. Bei der Pforte des Klosters taucht man vom Tageslärm in die Stille des Kreuzgangs ein, dessen frühgotisches Maßwerk aus dem 13. Jahrhundert stammt, als die Franziskaner hier zu bauen begannen. Von hier aus besuchten sie die Armen und Getretenen, um ihnen mit Predigt und Trost in ein christliches Leben zurückzuhelfen, von hier zogen sie in die Leprosenhäuser und pflegten die wegen ihrer ekelhaften Geschwüre aus der Stadt Ausgestoßenen, die nur einmal im Jahr durch die Stadt ziehen und betteln durften, nachdem sie mit Holzklappern die furchtsamen Bürger in die Häuser gescheucht hatten.

Die morgendliche Sonne steigt über die Hügel, die Würzburg im Kessel einfassen und behüten. Wie „Fühler von Insekten“ sah Heinrich von Kleist die spitzen Türme Würzburgs in den dunstigen Himmel stechen.

The sun slowly rises over the hills that surround and protect Würzburg in its hollow. Heinrich von Kleist wrote that the delicate church spires were like the feelers of insects that point upward into the livid sky.

Le soleil est par-dessus les collines qui enserrent et protègent Würzburg. Heinrich von Kleist comparait les flèches des églises à des antennes d'insectes transperçant le ciel blême.

Tilman Riemenschneider

Die Franziskanergasse Nr. 1 bewohnte einst Tilman Riemenschneider.

Dieser große Bildhauer konnte in Würzburg erst durch die Heirat mit der Witwe eines Goldschmiedemeisters Bürgerrecht und Meisterrecht erringen.

Insgesamt heiratete er dreimal , denn nur der Meister, dessen Ehefrau für Gesellen und Lehrlinge sorgte, durfte auch welche beschäftigen. In der Werkstatt im Hof wurden all' die vielfigurigen Altäre geplant und geschnitzt, die mit ihren Aposteln und Heiligen, der Trinität und Maria noch einmal die religiöse Welt des ausgehenden Mittelalters beschworen. Auch wenn die Gesellen die Gewandfalten schufen, Ochs und Esel, Stall und Krippe schnitzten, die Madonnen mit den zarten Gesichtern und die Heiligen mit den nervigen Händen behielt er sich vor. Die empfindsamen Frauen am Grab, die vom Verrat des Judas getroffenen Jünger, die melancholischen Marien atmen seinen Geist.

Riemenschneider, in Heiligenstadt auf dem Eichsfeld um 1460 geboren, in Osterode am Harz als Sohn eines Münzmeisters aufgewachsen, war kein sanfter Grübler. Er stand mitten im Leben, wurde in Würzburg in den Rat gewählt, besorgte dort verschiedene Ämter wie Fisch- und Spitalmeister, war ein Jahr lang auch einer der beiden Bürgermeister. Was ihn dazu trieb, die Sache der aufständischen Bauern zu vertreten, blieb unbekannt. Nach dem niedergeschlagenen Bauernaufstand büßte er die Hälfte seines Vermögens ein, und die geistliche Kundschaft wollte nichts mehr mit ihm zu schaffen haben. Er starb 1531 am Vortag von Kiliani. Am 7. Juli jeden Jahres wird daher im Auftrag des Stadtrates ein Kranz an der Kopie seines Grabsteins an der Nordwand des Doms niedergelegt.

Balthasar Neumann

Das Haus schräg gegenüber der Franziskanergasse Nr. 1, an der Ecke zur Wohlfahrtsgasse, tauschte Balthasar Neumann 1725 mit der Familie der Freiherren von Hutten. Von ihm zeugt nur noch das Torgewände mit Emblemen der Artillerie und der Balkon über dem Dach, wo er der Legende nach den Fortschritt der Arbeiten an der Residenz mit einem Fernglas verfolgt haben soll.

Hier entstanden die Pläne für die Wallfahrtskirchen Vierzehnheiligen und Gößweinstein, für die gewagten Treppenhäuser in Brühl und Bruchsal, auch für die Quellfassung des Rakoczibrunnens in der Saale zu Bad Kissingen, für eine Tauberbrücke, für Amtshäuser und Bürgerbauten. Häufig auf Reisen, nicht nur zu den eigenen Baustellen, sondern auch als gesuchter Berater in Trier und Ehrenbreitstein, Bonn und Ellwangen, reichte die verbliebene Arbeitszeit noch, an großen Wettbewerben für die Schlösser in Karlsruhe, Stuttgart und Wien teilzunehmen.

Als er 1753 mit militärischen Ehren in der Marienkapelle beigesetzt wurde, hatte Würzburg den Gestalter seines barocken Antlitzes verloren.

Würzburg

Metropolis on the Main

Wie mit Puderzucker überstäubt liegt die Altstadt zu Füßen der Festung, wenn einmal, selten genug, Schnee gefallen ist. Wohlige Ruhe breitet sich aus.

The Old Town at the foot of the Festung (fortress) looks like it has been sprinkled with powdered sugar when an occasional snow happens to fall on Würzburg. There is a peace and quiet in the air since all the traffic sounds have been muffled.

Quand par hasard il a neigé sur la Vieille Ville blottie au pied de la forteresse, elle semble toute saupoudrée de sucre et alors s'étend un silence ouaté que nul bruit de circulation ne transperce.

In Würzburg the stones speak volumes

It is not only the largest and most prestigious places in the world that are teeming of a past of grandeur and power, piety and the fear of death: narrow cobblestone streets, open courtyards and chapel cloisters can recount the episodes of a city's bygone days equally well. If you listen closely, they will retell the history of a city that more than once was on the brink of ruin, of a city that survived because it had the desire and willpower to do so.

Hear the raving and raging of the flagellants after the ghetto was burned to the ground, Hans Böhm's choking voice singing pious hymns on the funeral pyre, or take notice of the hefty disputing among the peasants in "Stachel" as they decide to storm the fortress Marienberg. Eavesdrop in on the Te Deum being sung by the Franciscans upon the founding of the university, pay attention to the plea to be spared as Swedish troops loot everything in sight, listen to the caterwauling of the Savoys beneath the Residenz windows until they are chased off, give an ear to the distinct shouts of joy as the first passenger train arrives in Würzburg, take heed of the heavy marching footsteps of soldiers in the streets and the Führer's speeches that blast from the loudspeakers and finally, hear the crackling of the firey red blaze that races through the streets. Würzburg is unique and its story worth telling.

It all began with a murder

History tells us that in 686 the wandering Irish bishop Kilian came with his companions Kolonat and Totnam to a settlement on the Main called Virteburh, which had been an official Frankish duchy since 630. Here, these apostles preached Christianity to the fishermen and shipbuilders who lived at the foot of the Marienberg as well as to the blacksmiths and carriage builders who worked for the duchy. But the words of the preachers fell on deaf ears – these dauntless people who were unwillung to compromise were not interested in lukewarm religious ideas.

When the apostles demanded that the duke divorce his wife because she had previously been married to his deceased brother – something their religion did not permit – Gailana, the duke's wife, knowing that she would be ousted from the duchy, had the apostles killed and buried under some horse stables. This martyrdom instilled deep religious belief in the people and missionaries began coming regularly to the settlement.

In 752 some persistent horses pawed their stable floor so indefatigably that the remains of the three were discovered whereupon they were taken to the Marienkirche (Mary's Church) for safety purposes and later moved to their present resting place in the Neumünster Church. Pilgrims soon started to flock to the crypt, especially on the 8th of July, Kilian's Name Day. Charlemagne led a pilgrim procession to the grave in 788 and in 793 sought comfort and renewed strength in front of the relics. He felt special kinship towards this saint because he hoped to see the entire east Frankish empire united under Kilian's grace. In addition, the spring water from the nearby well was said to heal or at least linder the pain of eye disorders. The multitudes that thronged to the holy site made it necessary to display the costly skull coverings and relics of the martyrs on the steps of the Cathedral.

High Mass is accompanied by a Fair

The pilgrims who came from far and wide to celebrate High Mass needed, above all, refreshment and candles that were not to be had in the outlying villages. A lively trade began under the protection of the bishop having the right to coin money and charge a ferry tax as well as hold a daily market and a yearly fair during the octave of Kilian which was just before the peasants went off to their fall harvests. The annual fair was held between the Cathedral steps and the Old Main Bridge – the entire Domstrasse was bustling with booths and street space and archways could be rented from the street's inhabitants for a handsome sum.

Such a fair attracted more than just the pious; jugglers, acrobats and tightrope artists performed for a hunk of bread or a piece of cheese. Quack doctors pulled teeth for a copper coin. A sharp eye was kept on beggars and gypsies, a disrespectable folk who had no permanent home or trade.

Over the years the fair often changed its appearance; it was slowly forced out of the town until it found its present place on the Talavera. Yet a desire for excitment and adventure and the unusual has kept people coming back. Nowadays, it is the rollercoasters or the huge Ferris wheel along with the looping rides and fireworks that cause that certain tingle. Everyone gathers in the enormous beer tent when the Lord Mayor officially opens the fair by tapping the first keg of fair beer.

Wine and other Festivals

The origin of the wine festivals in Würzburg goes back to the times when the knightly charitable institution St. Burkard was permitted to sell wine for half price during the first 3 days of the octave of Kilian. After the First World War, a wine festival was held on Michaelmas (September 29) in order to have enough empty vats for the new crop of grapes and, of course, to enable wine connoissuers everywhere to enjoy a good glass of wine. The fact that many local inhabitants hated having to wait until September for such a noble drop to drink gave way to the idea of a wine village held at the Market Place in May when food, drink and socializing can be harmoniously united. The Bürgerspital and the the state-owned wine cellars follow suit in June. As of May 1988, beer lovers also managed to exert their rights and can also enjoy a light or dark pint during the annual beer festival.

The Lusamgärtchen (The Lusam Garden)

In May 1883 several old houses near the Neumünster Church were torn down in order to dig the foundations for a department store. Thereby, the northern arcade side of the Neumünster cloisters which have been dated early 13th century or even 1170/80 was discovered. The fragments were put in safe keeping until 1908 when the owner was paid 75000 marks by a museum in Berlin for this Hohenstaufen architecture and sculpture. Local citizens were enraged and the Prince-Regent intervened to put a halt to the transaction. The cloisters wing was put on display in the Würzburg city museum in 1912 where it remained until after the bombings of the Second World War. In 1953 it was set up on the south side of the tiny Lusam Garden in which canons once read their breviaries. If they happened to look up during their meditation, their gaze fell upon the relief of Christ seated on a throne holding the Gospels. If their glance was cast at their feet, they saw the effigies of their predecessors.

Walther von der Vogelweide

Walther von der Vogelweide, the 13th century minnesinger, lies buried in the Lusam Garden as well. In 1219/20 Emperor Frederick II bestowed upon him an ecclesiastical benefice that allowed him to spend his later days at the collegiate church Neumünster. Walther was so pleased to have a permanent roof over his head that he set his jubilation to verse: I have my benefice! Hear me world, I have my benefice! I no longer need to fear frostbitten toes! The noble king, the generous king has taken care of me so that a breeze will cool my summers and a hot fire warm my winters.

This joy arose from the fact that Walther von der Vogelweide had spent his life wandering from one royal court to another – from Vienna to Eisenach and even further; more than once parched with thirst, cold and threadbare. He was the German language's most renowned minnesinger but he was more: he composed poignant political songs against popes and the curia. At one moment he was on the side of Hohenstaufen, the next moment he had switched over to the side of the Guelphs, and finally, his loyality was dedicated to the young Hohenstaufen Frederick II.

In 1930 Würzburg celebrated the 700th anniversary of Walther's death. Flat basins were chiselled out at the corners of the memorial in order to fulfill a last wish of the minnesinger, namely, that the birds should always find reason to pause at his grave for a drink. The inscription around the stone is handed down from the early 14th century and reads: Here lies Walther von der Vogelweide, he who forgets me, does me injustice. Alongside the numerous visitors, it is not unusual to find fresh flowers and chirping birds at his grave.

Max Dauthendey
torn between home and afar

When his remains were brought back to Würzburg from Java in 1923, he was laid to rest near the cloisters wall of the Neumünster. Later, his casket was moved to the family grave at the Central Cemetery where he was placed at the side of his father under whom he had suffered almost a lifetime. He dealt with this love-hate relationship that drove him to the far corners of the earth in "Der Geist meines Vaters" ("In the Spirit of my Father") in 1912 at the age of 45. He first ran away from home when he was 13 but only got as far as Aschaffenburg. Later, he crossed the "Seven Seas" but his homesickness always called him back: "When he heard the roosters crowing at the market in Paris, his thoughts immediately wandered off to the crowing cocks in the Franconian villages. And where the jungle meets the beaches in Mexico, he felt as if the sunny, vineyard-covered hills of the Main valley and the towers of his home town were close by" (Max Rößler). His trips through Asia provided him with material for his 12 Asiatic novellas and his novella "Die acht Gesichter am Biwasee) (1911) marked the beginning of a friendship that eventually led to the partnership between the Japanese city of Otsu on Lake Biwa and Würzburg in 1979. Although a successful author, Dauthendey was always in debt to such an extent that in 1914 he had to disappear in the Far East. Surprised by the First World War, he was interned on Java and thus separated from his wife and homeland for four years. Weary of the Tropics, he wrote his wife: "I walk through the incense-filled churches of Würzburg and attend matin with you and then we visit the manger scene at the Käppele on the Niklausberg and look down onto the windows of our apartment on the Main where the sparrows are waiting to be fed on the cold window sills."

Dauthendey died a homesick man in Melang, Java on August 29, 1918, just 72 days before the end of the war.

Leonard Frank
for peace and against violence

Leonard Frank, born as the son of a carpenter's apprentice in the Main quarter in 1882, suffered considerably during his school days under the tyranny of a teacher whose pedagogic methods consisted mainly of petrifying his pupils with cynicism and beatings. In his second book "Die Ursache" ("The Reason") which is a vehement plea against the death penalty, he gets even with this teacher. Leonard tried his hand at working in a laboratory, at chauffeuring and painting before he received a scholarship which enabled him to study at the Art Academy in Munich. In Berlin with his young wife and hardly able to make ends meet, he overcame the inner pain of his youth by depicting the desires and oppressions of himself and his companions in the "Räuberbande" ("Band of Robbers") (1914). It took him three months to write the first half page after which he felt himself released from the feelings he had kept pent-up inside himself for so many years. The book ends with the words: The evening sun shone over the city. A red ball of clouds lay over the grey fortress and on the steep vineyard slopes below it, the white head-scarves of the wine-growers glistened – the grape harvest had begun. The air smelled of water, tar, and incense.

When the First World War broke out, this man of pacifist conviction emigrated to Zurich and joined a pacifist group for whose "Weiße Blätter" magazine he wrote short stories condemning war and violence. His collection of short stories "Der Mensch ist gut" ("Man is Good") was smuggled into Germany in 1917/18 in the hopes that the human slaughtering going on could be stopped at least one day earlier. Frank returned to Germany in 1918 where he wrote sequels to his "Räuberbande". In addition he wrote the homecoming tragedy "Karl und Anna" which stirred up a small sensation as a play and a film. When Hilter came to power and had Frank's books burned, he fled via Switzerland to France. Although his citizenship had been revoked, when France entered the war, the French interned him. He was able to flee just in the nick of time as German troops were taking over the internment camp. In Hollywood he wrote "The German Novella", a psychological study of subordination. Suffering from the shock of having seen a photo of bombed-out Würzburg, Frank wrote "The Disciples of Christ", a novel which described postwar Würzburg and which was misinterpreted as being reality. Upon his return to Munich, he wrote his autobiography "Links wo das Herz ist" ("On the Left, Where the Heart is") in which he formulated his ideas and hopes for a just, socialist economic order. Frank died in Munich in 1961.

Aus dem Dunst hebt sich silbergrau die Silhouette der Stadt. Steil ragt der Turm der Neubaukirche auf, ruhig liegt der Dom wie ein Schiff neben der Kuppel von Neumünster. Im Vordergrund steht beharrlich Petrinis Kirche Stift Haug mit den dreimal gekuppelten Türmen.

The silhouette of the city rises above the silver-grey mist. The steeple of the Neubaukirche soars straight up, the Cathedral with its four towers rests like a giant ship next to the dome of the Neumünster. Petrini's Stift Haug Church with triple domed towers stands steadfast in the foreground.

La silhouette argentée de la ville se détache sur fond de brume. La tour de la Neubaukirche s'élance dans le ciel alors que la cathédrale aux quatre tours ressemble à un immense navire auprès de la coupole de l'église adjacente Neumünster. Au premier plan, l'église Stift Haug, de Pétrini, avec ses coupoles étagées semble ancrée pour l'éternité.

The Theater in Würzburg

The secularization in 1802/03 brought about Würzburg's annexation to Bavaria and with it, the great spiritual sellout. The Residenz and its wine cellars were turned over to the state while the Cathedral canons were put up for sale; monstrances, chalices and patens were melted down in the royal mint in Munich and jewels were auctioned off as Munich, the capital, was in dire need of money to pay its soldiers in order to acquire even more bishoprics and Imperial cities. But the new rulers did not stop there: they regulated the number of candles to be lit at High Mass, the number of mourners to participate in a funeral procession as well as the number of people that could be present at a baptismal feast. Crèches, pilgrimages and alms for the poor were strictly forbidden.

This secularization, however, had its good side too. Narrow-minded censorships were abolished and once again, there was ready access to the works of Goethe and Lessing. The world of the theater was no longer limited to traveling theater groups who performed edifying plays or buffoonery only a few days a year. In record time a charitable institution on Theaterstrasse was converted into a permanent theater seating 700. The "Electoral Franconian National Theater" performed "Still Waters Run Deep" on August 3, 1804, and only five days later, Mozart's "Escape from the Seralgio". The theater with its plush burgundy red seating and luxurious ornamentation in alabaster with gilded trimming performed the classics that had too long been removed from the stages of southern Germany. Mozart was extremely popular, especially during the reign (1804-16) of the Grand Duke of Toscany who was a generous patron and an avid theater-goer in Würzburg. The theater presented the well-established plays of the period and on the days when no performances were held, acrobats or brass bands were permitted to demonstrate their talents. Despite extensive efforts to please Würzburg audiences, the private theater was forced to close its doors in 1849: The death of the theater patroness, Karoline, the widow of the king, and the week of mourning in which no performances were scheduled plus numerous political gatherings as a result of the revolution that held the public's interest moreso than stage productions were the culminating factors that caused the director to resign and take on a mediocre position as a civil servant. The state took over the theater. Richard Wagner was first performed in Würzburg to an enthusiastic audience in 1864. A little over a hundred years later (1966), Wagner's "Meistersänger" would be performed on the opening night of the new city theater.

A School of Music

The annexation of Würzburg to Bavaria made it possible for the 21-year old law student, Franz Joseph Fröhlich, to become the director of an academic music society in 1801. The state had turned this society into a music institute, which, after its counterpart in Berlin, is the second oldest institute of its kind in Germany. At first only professionals were admitted but soon afterwards, the institute's doors were opened to anyone who could qualify.

Dr. Fröhlich was made a tenured professor in 1811 and held lectures in philosophy, didactics and pedagogy. He also gave violin and voice lessons to future teachers and earned a little on the side by giving private organ lessons. Fröhlich took his most gifted students and put together an orchestra that performed during the winter semester. A Prussian medical student, upon hearing a concert in the former chapter room of the Cathedral, wrote home to Potsdam how expertly contemporary composers were being interpreted in Würzburg. This chapter room emblazoned with 387 canon crests was not the only concert hall in Würzburg; the "Harmony" Society, fomerly a reading club, had a magnificent concert hall built in the canon courtyard of the Rannenburg (Hofstrasse 3). Guest artists appeared here on a regular basis and lively competition developed between the Harmony Society and the Royal School of Music as to who could engage the most renowned soloists and orchestra conductors.

After Hermann Zilcher became the head of the State Conservatory for Music in 1920, he called to life the idea of a Mozart Festival to be held in the Emperor's Hall of the Residenz which had been opened to the public after the withdrawal of the Wittelsbacher kings. A Mozart Festival has been held every year since 1920 with only two interruptions. One was during the war-torn years immediately following World War II and the other was the period in which the columns in the vestibule of the Residenz had to be replaced. Balthasar Neumann could not have foreseen that these columns would have to support the weight of the White Hall for more than 200 years. Soloists and the orchestra from the university's School of Music still perform at the Mozart Festival every June.

The Fascination of the narrow Franziskanergasse (Franciscan Street)

An admirer of Würzburg advises visitors to take a look at more than just those sights that have earned two stars in Baedeker. There ist more to be seen and a good place to start discovering on one's own is in the picturesque, narrow streets that offer an enchantment all their own. The Franziskanergasse is one of these streets. The portal gate to the monastery leads into the early Gothic cloisters that seem far-removed from the noise of the busy streets. Here in the 13th century, the Franciscans began their missionary work of teaching the word of God and helping the needy and of consoling the downtrodden. From here they went forth to care for and comfort the lepers who were condemned to live on the outskirts of Würzburg and who were allowed to come into the town only once a year in order to beg. The very sight of them wearing blinders to cover their deformities was enough to cause fearsome townsfolk to retreat to the safety of their own four walls.

Tilman Riemenschneider

Number 1 Franziskanergasse is the former home of Tilman Riemenschneider who through his marriage to the daughter of a local goldsmith acquired a house, a workshop complete with apprentices, town citizenship and the right to call himself a "master"craftsman all in one day. His wife's children and his children ensured a lively home life. In the course of his lifetime, Riemenschneider would have to repeat these marriage vows three more times because at that time a master craftsman was only allowed to keep apprentices if he had a wife that could feed them. It was in the workshop in this courtyard that all of his splendid altars were designed and carved – works that show the apostles, the Trinity and the Virgin in a manner characteristic of the waning Middle Ages. Even though his apprentices often carried out the carving of the folds in the garments or of the oxen and donkeys in the manger, it was Riemschneider alone who created the delicate features of the madonnas and the saints with their finely-veined hands. His gift for expressing grief and suffering is evident in his portrayal of the women gathered at the tomb, the disciples whose sorrow is visible in their every feature, and Mary, in mourning for her Son.

Tilman Riemenschneider, who was born in 1460 in Heiligenstadt and who grew up in Osterode at the edge of the Harz Mountains as the son of a minter, was anything but an introvert. He led a very active life, was elected to the town council, headed the Fisherman's Guild, was the overseer of the hospital, and for a year, he was even one of the town's two mayors. Just why he sided with the peasants during the Peasant's War remains unclear, but he paid heavily for this support – half of his fortune and his ecclesiastical customers. He died in 1531, a day before the beginning of the octave of St. Kilian. Each year on the 7th of July, the city council has a wreath placed on the replica of his tomb located on the north wall of the Cathedral.

Balthasar Neumann

In 1725 Balthasar Neumann traded the palace in which he had been living beyond his means for the more modest house on the corner of Franziskanergasse and Wohlfahrtsgasse. The only evidence of his residence there is the portal decoration of artillery emblems and the rooftop balcony where, as legend will have it, he stood and observed through a telescope the progress being made on the construction of the Residenz. In this house he drew up the plans for the pilgrimage churches Vierzehnheiligen and Goßweinstein; he also designed the striking staircases for Brühl and Bruchsal as well as came up with the plans for tapping spring water for the Rakoczi Fountain near Bad Kissingen. A bridge across the Tauber and various administrative buildings and patricians houses came to life in this narrow street. Neumann's time was occupied with visiting his construction sites, but moreso, with architectural consultations in Trier, Bonn and Ellwangen. When time permitted, he submitted plans for the construction of palaces in Karlsruhe, Stuttgart and Vienna. In 1753 Neumann was buried with military honors in Mary's Chapel at the Market Place. With his death the city lost the genius of a man who had transformed Würzburg into a Baroque city.

It is time for the visitor to depart on his own discovery of some of Würzburg's more pleasurable spots some of its churches and squares, its fountains and parks. A cool, refreshing "Schoppen" of Franconian wine is the best way to round out a day of sightseeing and become acquainted with the people who call Würzburg home.

Würzburg

Métropole au bord du Main

Über den gemächlich fließenden Main gleitet der Blick hinüber zur Festung Marienberg, die über den mächtigen Bastionsmauern beherrschend auf das Mainviertel blickt.

The eyes glance across the leisurely-flowing Main to the fortress Marienberg that majestically towers above the strong walls of the bastion.

La vue s'étend par delà le Main qui coule paresseusement; la forteresse Marienberg s'impose au-dessus des murs de soutien et règne sur le quartier de la rive gauche. La tour de Randersacker fait face à l'observateur.

Von abendlicher Sonne goldgelb umflossen, hebt sich die Turmkrone aus der winterlichen Stadt. Vor den Türmen des Doms und der breiten Kuppel von Neumünster steht der filigrane, schlanke Helm der Marienkapelle mit dem goldnen Marienbild.

In a blaze of light the crown of towers stands out in the night. The stone roof of the Marienkapelle with its gilded statue of Mary ascends in front of the four towers of the Cathedral and the tower and dome of the Neumünster.

La couronne des tours se détache sur le fond sombre de la ville. La flèche supportant la Vierge d'or de la Marienkapelle s'élance; à l'arrière plan les quatre tours de la cathédrale à côté du dôme de l'église Neumünster.

A Würzburg les pierres parlent.

Il n'y a pas que les bâtiments de renommée européenne qui nous parlent des puissants de ce monde, de grandeur, de piété ou de la peur de la mort, ce sont aussi les étroites ruelles, places, chapelles et monastères qui racontent, eux aussi, les épisodes de la vie d'une vieille ville qui, plusieurs fois au cours de son histoire, se trouva sur le point d'être détruite mais survécut, telle un phoenix renaissant de ses cendres.

Celui qui, cheminant à travers la Vieille Ville, sait prêter l'oreille entendra les flagellants après l'incendie du ghetto, comme il entendra Hans Böhm sur son bûcher chantant d'une voix étouffée des cantiques à la Vierge, et les chefs des paysans se quereller violemment dans la taverne «Stachel» avant de prendre la fatale décision d'attaquer la forteresse, il écoutera avec recueillement le Te Deum s'élevant de la chapelle des Franciscains après la fondation de la faculté, il entendra le peuple gémir et demander grâce lors du pillage des troupes suédoises et le charivari que les Savoyards faisaient sous les fenêtres de la Résidence avant que l'évêque ne les fassent reconduire aux frontières, il entendra les hourras à l'arrivée du premier train de voyageurs, le pas cadencé des soldats et les discours du Führer retransmis par des haut-parleurs criards puis finalement le souffle brûlant et le crépitement de la ville en flammes.

Je voudrais vous conduire hors des sentiers battus par les touristes, là où se fit notre histoire pour que vous appreniez et ressentiez en quoi cette ville est unique au monde.

Cela commença par un meurtre.

La légende veut que ce soit en 686 que l'évêque Kilian et ses compagnons Totnan et Kolonat s'établissent dans la bourgade de Virteburh, sise au bord du Main et depuis 630 propriété d'un duc franconien. C'est ici qu'ils prêcheront les bateliers et pêcheurs habitant le quartier situé au-dessous du château-fort aussi bien que les charrons et palefreniers qui logeaient sur la rive droite, mieux protégée des inondations, et où allait être construite la cathédrale par la suite. Ces Irlandais étaient durs et refusaient tant les compromis que la tiédeur de ceux qui, par habitude ou par lâcheté, tenaient encore aux anciens dieux. C'est ainsi qu'ils demandèrent au duc Gosbert, qu'ils avaient gagné à leur cause, de répudier sa femme Gailana, veuve de feu son frère: le droit canon refusant les mariages entre beau-frère et belle-soeur. Gailana, touchée dans son honneur et craignant de perdre toute influence en Franconie en cas de séparation, profita de ce que son époux guerroyait en Thuringe pour faire assassiner les évangélisateurs dont les corps furent enfouis à la hâte sous une écurie. La mort des martyrs, dont les ossement furent retrouvés en 752, renforça cependant la foi chrétienne et les reliques retrouvées furent d'abord transportées dans l'église de la forteresse qui semblait à Burkard, le premier évêque, l'endroit le plus sûr. Trois ans plus tard une procession solennelle les conduisit de nouveau sur la rive droite, dans la cathédrale du Rédempteur que Megingaud, qui avait succédé à Burkard, avait commencé de faire bâtir. Charlemagne encouragea les pélerinages, surtout à la Saint Kilian, le 8 juillet, pour que les Francs puissent élever leurs regards vers un saint reconnu et vénéré dans tout son empire. Il alla lui-même plusieurs fois se recueillir dans la crypte.

De la messe à la foire.

Les pélerins venus de loin assister aux offices religieux devaient se restaurer, ils voulaient également brûler et acheter des cierges et tout ce qu'on ne trouvait pas dans leurs villages. Pour protéger tous les boutiquiers, l'évêque Meginhard, comte de Rothenburg, obtint de l'Empereur Konrad II, en 1030, outre les droits de frapper monnaie, de lever un impôt sur le passage du fleuve et aux péages ainsi que de tenir chaque jour un marché, celui d'avoir une foire annuelle qui aurait lieu du 17 au 24 août. Comme la population paysanne était alors occupée aux moissons, la foire fut remise à la semaine de la Saint Kilian. Elle s'étendait des marches de la cathédrale au pont sur le Main, en suivant la rue de la cathédrale: la Domstrasse.

Et puis au plaisir.

Tant de personnes prêtes à dépenser leur argent attiraient inévitablement les saltimbanques, jongleurs, acrobates et montreurs d'ours, auxquels se mêlaient bien des gueux sans honneur, ni maison, ni métier. Les autorités avaient à l'oeil artistes et arracheurs de dents, mais aussi mendiants et juifs. La fête populaire changea plusieurs fois d'endroit et fut reléguée finalement sur la Talavera où, aujourd'hui encore, on rencontre les mêmes stands de tir, manèges et divertissements, mais en plus grand, plus rapide, plus effrayant encore; et l'audacieuse jeunesse réclame des sentations autrement plus violentes que la grande roue ou les montagnes russes. C'est l'énorme tente qui rassemble tous les amateurs de bière aux sons des flonflons quand le premier maire de la ville met traditionnellement en perce le premier tonneau de bière. Quand les deux feux d'artifices offerts par les forains éclatent dans le ciel au début et à la fin de la Fête de Kiliani, rares sont ceux qui pensent aux fusées qui, dans la nuit du 16 mars 1945, ont illuminé l'emplacement de la ville avant qu'un tapis de bombes ne la pilonne.

Fêtes du vin et autres.

A l'origine de toutes se trouve le droit que s'étaient fait accorder les chanoines de vendre à moitié prix leur vin les trois premiers jours de la semaine de la Saint Kilian, au grand dépit d'ailleurs des taverniers qui voyaient alors émigrer leur clientèle.

Après la première guerre mondiale, une fête de trois jours, commençant à la Saint Michel (29 septembre), devait aider à vider les tonneaux avant les nouvelles vendanges. Mais certains voulant déjà cette joyeuse atmosphère dès le printemps, un «village du vin», aux nombreuses maisonnettes de dégustation se tient sur la place du marché depuis 1987. En juin, c'est le Bürgerspital qui régale les Würzbourgeois et les touristes dans la cour pittoresque de son hospice; une semaine plus tard les vignobles d'Etat font apprécier leurs vins sous les arbres du jardin de la Résidence.

Les amateurs de bière ne voulant pas être en reste, les brasseurs de Basse-Franconie leur offrent des blondes ou des brunes, au choix, depuis mai 1988.

Mainabwärts gleitet unser Schiff. Rückblickend betrachten wir das Kloster Oberzell im barocken Gewand. Im morgendlichen Schleier verschwinden Stahltanks vom Neuen Hafen an der Grenze der Stadt.

Our ship glides downstream. Looking back we see the Cloister Oberzell garbed in Baroque alongside the concrete blocks of buildings and steel tanks of the Neuen Hafen (New Harbor).

Notre bateau descend le Main et, en nous retournant, nous voyons, aux limites de la ville, le monastère Oberzell dont le style baroque contraste avec les citernes métalliques et les blocs de ciment du Nouveau Port (Neuhafen).

Le petit jardin «Lusamgärtchen».

Quand en mai 1883 Salomon Rosenthal entreprit des travaux pour agrandir les caves de son magasin, on découvrit la rangée d'arcades du cloître de Neumünster qui dateraient du XIIIième, de 1170-1180 selon d'autres même. Alarmé par la population de Würzburg qui craignait que les précieux fragments ne soient transférés dans un musée berlinois, le Prince-Régent Luitpold les racheta. Après les destructions de la seconde guerre mondiale, ils furent installés dans le petit jardin Lusam où autrefois les chanoines déambulaient en lisant leur bréviaire ou en contemplant soit les pierres tombales de leur prédécesseurs, soit les bas-reliefs de ces piliers.

Les notices de Michael de Leone, chef de la chancellerie épiscopale nous apprennent que dans cette cour est enterré Walther von der Vogelweide, le plus grand troubadour de langue allemande qui put ici, grâce à l'Empereur Frédéric II, trouver un revenu pour ses vieux jours après avoir, toute sa vie durant, parcouru les grands chemins, allant de château impérial en château impérial avec Philippe de Souabe, un Hohenstaufen, tout d'abord, puis il fut invité par l'évêque Wolfger de Passau, après quoi il se retrouva du côté de guelfes qu'il quittera finalement pour accueillir le jeune Frédéric II, ce qui valut au quinquagénaire qu'il était devenu entre temps une trêve de dix années pendant lesquelles il écrivit les «Elégies» et la «Chanson des Croisades». Lorsqu'en 1930, pour célébrer le sept centième anniversaire présumé de sa mort, la ville de Würzburg lui fit ériger une pierre tombale, on n'omit point d'en incurver les quatre angles pour permettre aux oiseaux de s'y abreuver, selon un souhait du ménestrel que la tradition a transmis. Les visiteurs ne manquent pas non plus d'y déposer régulièrement des fleurs.

Max Dauthendey
déchiré entre le mal du pays et l'appel du large.

Avant de trouver la paix éternelle au cimetière de Würzburg à côté de son père, un photographe qui avait émigré de St Petersbourg, Max Dauthendey avait parcouru le monde sans cesser de penser à sa Franconie natale. Ses nombreux voyages en Asie lui inspirèrent des recueils de nouvelles. «Les huit visages du lac Biwa» ammèneront en 1979 le jumelage de la ville de Würzburg avec la ville japonaise d'Otsu au bord du lac Biwa. Surpris au fin fond de l'Asie par la première guerre mondiale, incarcéré à Java, il y mourut en août 1918 avec en pensée devant les yeux: «Les vielles églises, bleues d'encens, de Würzburg.»

Leonhard Frank
pour la paix et contre la violence.

Le fils d'un menuisier, né en 1882 dans le quartier du Main, souffrit toute sa scolarité des coups et sarcasmes d'un instituteur tyrannique. Après avoir interrompu un dur apprentissage, il gagna sa vie comme aide-laborantin, chauffeur, peintre en bâtiment, puis reçut une bourse pour l'Académie des Beaux Arts à Munich. Il mena ensuite une vie de misère avec sa jeune femme à Berlin où il écrivit en 1914 le premier tome de sa trilogie franconienne, terminée à son retour en Allemagne après la guerre. S'il mit trois mois pour en écrire la première demi-page, il trouva et garda ensuite le rythme et le style concis qui lui permirent de se libérer et de guérir des blessures morales de sa jeunesse. Son livre «Karl et Anna», histoire d'amour tragique entre une femme et un homme qui revient de captivité – dont furent tirés une pièce de théâtre et un film – connut un énorme succès mais cela n'empêcha pas qu'à l'arrivée au pouvoir d'Hitler ses livres ne soient brûlés. Il réussit à émigrer en France, puis aux Etats Unis. Ce pacifiste convaincu mourut en 1961 à Munich après avoir terminé le roman autobiographique «A gauche, là où est le coeur» dans lequel il n'a toujours pas perdu l'espoir en un ordre juste et socialiste.

Un endroit de «joie et culture».

Quand la Bavière occupa Würzburg pour la première fois, en 1802-1803, l'Etat se réserva la Résidence et tous les vignobles du clergé et mit en vente aux enchères les biens de ce dernier. Ostensoirs, calices et patènes partirent à la Monnaie Royale: on avait besoin à Munich de payer les soldats et mercenaires qui, aux côtés de Napoléon, allaient mettre le grappin sur encore plus de comtés, villes impériales et biens collégiaux. Si le nouveau gouvernement alla jusqu'à réglementer les moindres rites éclésiastiques, il abolit aussi la censure, libérant ainsi les oeuvres de Goethe, Wieland et Lessing. Les Würzbourgeois qui jusqu'alors avaient dû se contenter des mélodrames et bouffonneries joués par les troupes ambulantes de passage pour quelques jours, eurent le droit de construire un théâtre où allaient se jouer pièces et opéras. En un temps record on aménagea un bâtiment sis Theaterstrasse en un théâtre de 700 places, aux sièges bordeaux contrastant avec les galeries or et blanches. «L'enlèvement au sérail» y fut le premier opéra représenté, suivi d'oeuvres de Lortzing, Weber puis Rossini et Donizetti.

Dès 1864 on y représenta les oeuvres de Wagner qui reçurent un accueil si chaleureux du public qui allait lui rester fidèle, qu'on choisit «Les maîtres chanteurs» pour la réouverture du théâtre au mois de décembre 1966. Le théâtre municipal d'aujourd'hui nous charme, nous fait passer un bon moment, nous provoque et nous incite à réfléchir, tout comme il y a 185 ans.

Une lettre envoyée en 1852 par un étudiant en médecine prussien à Potsdam fait part de la haute qualité d'interprétation des compositeurs modernes par un orchestre de solistes talentueux recrutés par Franz Joseph Fröhlich, qui était en grande concurrence avec «L'Harmonie» pour attirer à Würzburg solistes et maîtres de chapelle de renom.

Après avoir pris en 1920 la direction du Conservatoire, le Professeur Hermann Zilcher eut l'idée d'instaurer un festival Mozart dans la salle de l'Empereur de la Résidence. Depuis cette époque, mis à part deux interruptions immédiatement après la guerre et lors de la réfection d'un pilier, le festival a eu lieu chaque année, et chaque année des solistes et l'ochestre du conservatoire (Hochschule für Musik) y jouent à cette occasion des oeuvres de Mozart.

Du charme d'une ruelle,
la «Franziskanergasse».

Josef Hofmiller, un admirateur bavarois de Würzburg, nous conseille de partir à l'aventure, par les ruelles pittoresques, à la recherche des autres curiosités que celles qui ont reçu deux étoiles au Baedeker, que l'étranger doit découvrir lui-même et dont il n'oubliera plus le charme étrange.

La Franziskanergasse est une de ces ruelles pleine de surprises. On quitte le bruit de la ville en poussant la porte du cloître des Franciscains qui date du XIIIième siècle. C'est de là qu'ils allaient prêcher, consoler et soigner les pauvres et les lépreux.

Tilman Riemenschneider

Au numéro 1 habitait Tilman Riemenschneider, qui en épousant la veuve d'un orfèvre, avait acquis en un jour une maison, un atelier avec des ouvriers, les titres et droits de citoyen de la ville, mais aussi des enfants et une famille qui allait encore s'agrandir. Il dut d'ailleurs se remarier encore trois fois car seul pouvait employer des compagnons et apprentis le maître dont la femme pouvait s'en occuper. Même si ce sont ses ouvriers qui taillaient les plis des vêtements, le boeuf et l'âne, l'étable et la crèche, le maître se réservait les madones au fin visage ou les saints aux mains nerveuses et c'est de cette cour que sortirent les autels aux nombreux personnages, les apôtres et les saints qui sont les ultimes fleurons du Moyen Age qui se terminait alors. Riemenschneider n'était pas seulement un doux rêveur mais aussi un homme d'action. Elu au conseil, il fut une année durant l'un des deux maires de la ville. On ne sait ce qui le poussa à prendre fait et cause pour les paysans, mais cela lui coûta la moitié de ses biens et toute sa clientèle ecclésiastique. Il mourut en 1531 et chaque année, le jour anniversaire de sa mort, le conseil municipal fait déposer à la cathédrale une couronne sur la copie de sa pierre tombale.

Balthasar Neumann

En 1725 Balthasar Neumann échangea son palais de la Kapuzinerstrasse 2, qu'il avait génialement vu trop grand pour ses moyens, contre la maison d'angle au coin de la Wohlfahrtsgasse. De lui ne restent que son emblème au portail et le balcon sur le toit. La légende veut qu' il ait observé de là, à la lorgnette, les progrès de la construction de la Résidence. Mais c'est bien ici qu'il conçut les plans pour les églises de Vierzehnheiligen et Gössweinstein, les hardis escaliers de Brühl et Bruchsal et tant d'autres chefs-d'oeuvre. Lorsqu'il fut enseveli avec les honneurs militaires en 1753 dans la Marienkapelle, Würzburg avait perdu celui qui avait donné à la ville son caractère baroque.

Maintenant c'est à vous de partir découvrir Würzburg, ses ruelles et ses places, ses églises et ses monuments, ses fontaines et ses espaces verts. Et quand, fatigués, vous reprendrez des forces en dégustant un petit verre de son vin, alors découvrez le charme de ses habitants, car une ville ne vit que par ceux qui y demeurent.

Residenz

Schloß unter den Schlössern

Im geometrisch angelegten Garten vor der Südfront der Residenz ließ Fürstbischof Adam Friedrich von Seinsheim zwei Figurengruppen Johann Peter Wagners setzen. Direkt vor uns schleppt Hades Persephone, die Tochter des Zeus und der Demeter, in sein dunkles Reich.

Friedrich von Seinsheim had two groups of statues by Johann Peter Wagner placed in the geometrically laid out garden in front of the south entrance of the Residenz. In front of the rondel with the Toscanasaal, Zeus in the figure of Taurus abducts Europe to Crete; directly in front, Hades abducts the daughter of Zeus and Demeter, Proserpine, into the lower world.

Le prince-évêque Adam Friedrich von Seinsheim fit ériger deux groupes de statues dans l'ordonnance géométrique des jardins à la française devant l'aile sud de la Résidence. Directement devant nous, Hades enlève Perséphone, fille de Zeus et de Déméter, pour l'emmener dans son royaume des ombres.

Die Residenz sollte nicht nur dem Fürstbischof und seinem Hofstaat komfortable Unterkunft bieten und die Verwaltung des Hochstifts aufnehmen, sondern vor allem schon in ihrem Ausmaß und Aussehen von Reichtum und Bedeutung des geistlichen Staates künden. Ruhm und Ansehen der Familie Schönborn, die schon in der dritten Generation Kirchenfürsten stellte, waren auch noch treibende Kräfte zum Bau dieses Schlosses im Stil des Barock.

Die Pläne zur Residenz zu prüfen und zu koordinieren, die Vorstellungen des Bauherrn und eigene Ideen einzubringen war die Aufgabe Balthasar Neumanns, der auch bis zum Abschluß 1744 die Bauleitung inne hatte. Es zeugte von hohem Vertrauen des Fürstbischofs, daß er Planung und Bau des bedeutendsten Schlosses Süddeutschlands einem Mann anvertraute, der bis dahin erst drei Reihenhäuser im Mainviertel vorweisen konnte, von denen er eines selbst bewohnte. Mit 24 Jahren war Neumann 1711 als Geschützgießergeselle bei Kopp auf dem Schottenanger eingetreten, nahm, von einem Stipendium seiner Heimatstadt Eger unterstützt Unterricht in Geometrie, Feldmesserei und Architektur, entwarf einen Grundrißplan Würzburgs, nahm am Türkenfeldzug 1717 teil und sah sich auf dem Heimweg in Wien und Mailand um. Der Nordwestpavillon der Residenz wuchs bereits heran, da wollte der Bauherr nichts versäumen und schickte Neumann über Zabern und Nancy, wo Schlösser besehen wurden, nach Paris zu den führenden Architekten Robert de Cotte und Germain Boffrand. Während de Cotte fleißig an den Plänen strich, zeigte sich Boffrand vom Treppenhaus überzeugt und kam 1724 nach Würzburg, um sich zu unterrichten. Von de Cottes Streichungen war die der Hofkirche im nördlichen Oval angenehm; Neumann brachte sie ins Südwesteck. Als Boffrand kam, war der Bauherr plötzlich verstorben, von der Opposition der gelehrte Christoph Franz von Hutten gewählt worden, der den Bau einstellen ließ. Balthasar Neumann, zum Artillerie-Major befördert, konnte nur den unfertigen Nordblock unter Dach bringen.

Die Familie Schönborn, die den Bau der Residenz auch für eine Prestigefrage hielt, ließ Neumann nicht fallen. Kaum war 1729 der Reichsvizekanzler Friedrich Carl von Schönborn Bischof von Würzburg geworden, wurden die Arbeiten mit großem Elan wieder aufgenommen. Nun hatte es Neumann nur noch mit Lucas von Hildebrandt als Korrektor zu tun. 1737 war das riesige Treppenhaus fertig, 1739 der Kaisersaal begonnen. Als 1740 die Gartenfront vollendet war, begann man sofort mit der Ausstattung der Kaiserzimmer südlich des Kaisersaals. Im Dezember 1744 wurde ein Dankfest für die Vollendung gefeiert. Der Bauherr Friedrich Carl überlebte den Bau nur um zwei Jahre. Sein Nachfolger, der Alchemie verfallen, setzte Neumann ab, den 1749 Carl Philipp von Greiffenclau wieder einsetzte. Ihm gelang es mit Hilfe des Bankiers Mehling, der aus Würzburg stammte, den letzten großen Freskenmaler Venedigs, Giovanni Battista Tiepolo, mit seinen Söhnen nach Würzburg zu holen, „um seinen Namen und Kunst in Teutschland ebenmäßig zu verewigen". Nachdem die Fresken im Kaisersaal großartig ausgefallen waren, kam der Auftrag für das „Ausmalen" der Treppenhausdecke, mit 540 m^2 noch immer das größte Deckengemälde der Welt. Die restliche Ausstattung der Residenz zog sich unter Adam Friedrich von Seinsheim, einem Neffen der Schönbornbischöfe, bis 1774 hin. Schon 30 Jahre

Walther von der Vogelweide sitzt sinnend am Frankoniabrunnen, neben Tilman Riemenschneider, der an einer Figur schnitzt. Halb im Hintergrund Mathias Grünewald.

At the Franconiabrunnen (fountain) Walther von der Vogelweide contemplates how to gain and unite honor, property and God's grace in hard times while Tilman Riemenschneider carves a madonna. The artist, Mathias Grünewald, can be seen in the background.

Au pied de la fontaine Franconia le troubadour Walther von der Vogelweide est assis à côté du sculpteur Tilman Riemenschneider qui travaille à une madone et, à l'arrière plan, Mathias Grünewald.

WALTHER
V.D.VOGELWEIDE

später ließ Großherzog Ferdinand von Toskana im Südflügel Räume nach der neuesten Mode umgestalten, wovon noch der Toskanasaal zeugt.

Neumann gelang die Kombination zweier gegensätzlicher Schloßanlagen. Die beiden geschlossenen Vierflügelgebäude mit ihren zwei Binnenhöfen wurden so an den Quertrakt gehängt, daß ein tiefer Ehrenhof entstand. Zur Stadt hin war er durch ein geschwungenes Gitter abgeschlossen, das Hildebrandt entworfen und Johann Georg Oegg, der aus Silz/Tirol stammende Hofschlosser, in Eisen geschmiedet hatte. Kronprinz Ludwig ließ es 1821 meistbietend versteigern, um der Bevölkerung näher zu sein. Von den beiden Palais, die den Residenzplatz seitlich begrenzen, ziehen Arkaden zur Stadt hin, die von Johann Peter Wagner mit klassizistischen Figuren geschmückt wurden. Sie enden an Säulen, die vom Grünspan überzogene Kupferkugeln tragen. Ungefähr an der Stelle der einstigen Einfahrt in den Ehrenhof wurde 1894 der Frankoniabrunnen aufgestellt. Die Städte und Landkreise Unterfrankens hatten ihn zu Ehren des Prinzregenten Luitpold errichten lassen, der 1821 in der Residenz geboren wurde. Unter der Figur der Franconia und eines Medaillon des Prinzregenten sitzen die von Ferdinand von Miller d.J. gegossenen Figuren: Walther von der Vogelweide, Tilman Riemenschneider und Mathias Grünewald. Den Ehrenhof schließt das corps de logis ab, der Wohn- und Repräsentationsbau, der, um mehr Höhe für die Räume zu gewinnen, keine Halbgeschosse besitzt. Neumann hatte, damit vierspännig ins Vestibül ein- und ausgefahren werden konnte, drei mächtige Portale in den Mittelteil gefügt. Darüber empfangen die drei hohen Fenster des Weißen Saales ihr Licht von Westen. Von hier konnte Friedrich Carl von Schönborn direkt auf die Schönbornkapelle, die Grablege am Dom, sehen und, im Barock nicht außergewöhnlich, mitten im Leben an den Tod erinnert werden. Über den Fenstern prangt sein großes vielfeldriges Wappen, flankiert von zwei steinernen Engeln, die seinen Ruhm hinausposaunen. Übers Wappen durfte die Kaiserkrone gelegt werden, da er als Bischof von Bamberg das von Kaiser Heinrich II. gegründete Hochstift innehatte. Auf dem schieferblauen Dach schwingt sich der vergoldete Reichsadler auf.

Im niedrigen Vestibül, dessen vier massige Pfeiler von Atlanten des Johann Wolfgang van der Auwera mitgetragen werden, wurde eine Kuppel vorgetäuscht, die Franz Anton Ermeltraut Grau in Grau mit vier Taten des Herkules schmückte. In den Nischen der Südwand stehen seit 1779 Johann Peter Wagners Marmorstatuen der städteverwüstenden Kriegsgöttin Bellona und der Minerva (Athena), Göttin des Verstandes und Schutzherrin der Künste. Adam Friedrich von Seinsheim, der Auftraggeber, der in seinem Bistum Bamberg die Schäden des Siebenjährigen Krieges lindern mußte, stellte jedem allegorisch die Widersacher Vernunft und Zerstörung vor.

In den Laubengängen streiten und versöhnen sich die Putten Johann Peter Wagners (links). Auf der Balustrade an der Treppe zum Wall stehen Savoyardenknaben, die als kleine Musikantengruppen durch die Lande zogen, während ihre Väter als Hausierer mit dem Verkauf von Heilsalben und Seidenbändern sich vor dem Hunger bewahrten.

Johann Peter Wagner's putti angels quarrel and make up along the arbor paths. On the balustrade along the steps to the wall are the child musicians of the Savoy who used to accompany their fathers through the countryside while they peddled treacle and silk ribbons to keep themselves from starving.

Les amours de Johann Peter Wagner se font la nique et se réconcilient sous les tonnelles alors que, sur la balustrade de l'escalier qui monte aux remparts, les petits Savoyards musiciens vont de ville en ville gagner une pitance que leurs pères essayent d'obtenir en vendant de porte en porte des remèdes et des rubans de soie pour ne point mourir de faim.

Herbstliche Impressionen. Der englische Gartenstil, der am Ende des 18. Jahrhunderts in Mode kam, durchbricht mit seinen unbekümmert wachsenden Bäumen die klaren geometrischen Formen im Hofgarten.

Unkept trees, typical of the English Garden that became popular at the end of the 18th century, suddenly appear in the park whose dead-straight paths are otherwise bordered by neatly sculpted hedges and trees.

Impressions d'automne. Dans le parterre avec ses allées rectilignes, ses arbres et ses buissons taillés au cordeau, vient se heurter le style des jardins anglais qui devient à la mode à la fin du XVIIIième avec ses arbres qui, semble-t-il, poussent comme ils veulent.

Von hier führt der lichte, aber kühle Gartensaal zum Hofgarten. Hier hielt sich der Fürstbischof mit seinen Hofkavalieren an heißen Tagen auf, die man aus Termingründen nicht in Werneck oder Veitshöchheim zubringen konnte. Hier spazierte man im Umgang, den Neumann durch zwölf freistehende Marmorsäulen geschaffen hatte, und besah die Deckengemälde des Johannes Zick. In sinnenfroh kräftiger Art malte er zum Garten hin das „Mahl der Götter", denen Musik die Tafelfreuden erhöht. Zum Vestibül hin prangt die „Rast der Diana", deren Jagdgehilfen grün gewandet sind wie die des Fürstbischofs Carl Philipp von Greiffenclau. Er entließ Zick nach dieser „Talentprobe" und konnte Tiepolo verpflichten.

Das freitragende Muldengewölbe, mit dem Neumann gegen den Einspruch Hildebrandts das Treppenhaus überspannte, ertrug Dachstuhlbrände und den glühenden, dann nassen Schutt nach dem 16. März 1945. Da Tiepolo in den feuchten Sumpfkalk gemalt hatte, konnte sein Werk, gereinigt und stabilisiert, in den alten Farben leuchten; die Trockenmalerei der Hofkirche blieb lädiert. Neumann († 1753) erlebte noch, daß dieses riesige Fresko von Tiepolo und seinen Söhnen Domenico und Lorenzo von August 1752 bis Oktober 1753 unter großen Strapazen gemalt wurde, denn der Maler lag auf dem Gerüst auf dem Rücken und mußte in den frisch aufgetragenen Kalk malen, ohne Abstand vom Bild gewinnen zu können.

Schreitet man die flachen Stufen der Treppe zum Podest hinauf, rückt die farbenprächtige Darstellung des Erdteils Amerika näher, verkörpert durch eine Indianerin mit Federschmuck auf dem Haupt, die auf einem Alligator reitet. Steigt man nun auf einem der zwei Treppenläufe zum Weißen Saal empor, erblickt man Europa, den Kontinent der Künste und Wissenschaften. Dort sitzt Balthasar Neumann in der Uniform eines Obersten der fränkischen Kreisartillerie auf einem Kanonenrohr. Rechts von ihm steht, in einen hellgelben Mantel gehüllt, der Stukkateur Antonio Bossi, schon von Schwermut gezeichnet. Battista Tiepolo, der Schöpfer der Fresken aber schaut, die schützende Malermütze auf dem Kopf, links neben der Kartusche hervor, von seinem Sohn Domenico und dem Wiener Maler Franz Ignaz Roth begleitet.

Auf der Längsseite zur Stadt hin wird der Erdteil Asien dargestellt, verkörpert durch eine weißgekleidete Inderin auf einem Elefanten. Im düsteren Hintergrund stehen die drei Kreuze auf Golgatha, gestürzt ist die Figur Diana zu Ephesus, was den Sieg des Kreuzes über die Heidenschaft ausdrücken soll. Gegenüber reitet Afrika als Mohrenfürstin auf reich beladenem Kamel, gefolgt von Mohren und Negerhäuptlingen. Die vielen Gestalten sind alle gedeutet worden. Besonders die Farben sind es, die mal kräftig, mal in hauchdünnen Übergängen Landschaften und Menschen aufleuchten und lebendig werden lassen.

Über dem Kontinent Europa wird im hermelingefütterten Purpurmantel, von spielenden Putten begleitet, das Medaillon mit dem Abbild des Fürstbischofs Carl Philipp von Greiffenclau emporgetragen von der Fanfare blasenden Fama (Sinnbild des Ruhmes) und der lorbeerbekränzten Allegorie der Virtus (Tugend und Ehre), die ihm den Fürstenhut aufsetzt. Von Planetengöttern des gestirnten Himmels, von Luna, der Göttin der Nacht, entfernt sich Merkur (Hermes), der Beschützer des Handels und Mehrer des Wohlstands. Über Amerika aber geht leuchtend die Sonne auf, verkörpert

Während die Allegorien von Afrika und Asien die Längsseiten des größten Deckengemäldes der Welt füllen, hat Giovanni Battista Tiepolo an der Südseite Europa freskiert. Als hochgeachteter und hochbezahlter Künstler konnte er es wagen, an die wichtigste Stelle (in der Mitte oben rechts) Balthasar Neumann zu plazieren.

While the allegories of Africa and Asia occupy two sides of the world's largest ceiling painting, Giovanni Battista Tiepolo painted Europe in the frescos on the south side. As a highly-esteemed and well-paid artist, he could afford to place Balthasar Neumann in the center of the activities.

Alors que les allégories de l'Afrique et l'Asie ornent les grands côtés de la vaste fresque de la voûte autoportée, Giovanni Battista Tiepolo a réservé le côté sud pour l'Europe. Cet artiste renommé, et fort bien payé, pouvait se permettre de placer Balthasar Neumann à la place la plus importante.

Der Kaisersaal (links) ist nicht der einzige Höhepunkt der Residenz. Der Spiegelsaal und viele der Paradezimmer (Kaiserzimmer) prunken mit kostbaren Interieurs, die bis ins Detail von den Fürstbischöfen vorgeschlagen und kontrolliert wurden.

The Kaisersaal (Emperor's Hall) (left) shares its fame with the Spiegelsaal and many of the Imperial Apartments which exhibit great splendor throughout their interiors. These rooms were either decorated according to the specific instructions of the Prince-Bishops or were at least subject to their most scrutinous approval.

La salle de l'Empereur (Kaisersaal), à gauche, n'est pas le seul fleuron de la Résidence. La salle des glaces et de nombreuses pièces de parade (appartements de l'Empereur) rivalisent avec des intérieurs précieux dont les moindres détails furent contrôlés par les princes-évêques, quand ils ne les avaient pas proposés eux-mêmes.

von Apoll, dem Lichtgott und Beschützer der Künste. Er steigt, da ein neuer Tag anbricht, von seinem Tempel herab zu den angeschirrten Sonnenrossen, umgeben von Putten und Amoretten, Wind- und Stundengottheiten.

Zwei Türen führen in den Weißen Saal, zu fürstbischöflicher Zeit mal als Sommerspeise- oder Ballsaal, mal als Aufenthaltsraum der Leibgarde genutzt. Hier überzieht weißer Stuck, den Antonio Bossi 1744 auf grauem Grund auftrug, mit Kriegsemblemen, mit Muschel-, Blüten- und Tiermotiven filigran Gewölbe und Gewände. Gegen dieses jubelnde Rokoko setzte Materno Bossi, der Neffe, am Stuck des gußeisernen Ofens klassizistische Akzente. Fünf Kristallüster, um 1750 aus Wien beschafft, erhellen den Raum und die Bildnisse der Fürstbischöfe.

Nach Osten hin öffnet sich der Kaisersaal am vorspringenden Mittelteil der Gartenfront, das Herzstück der Residenz, 1742 gewölbt, aber erst 1751/52 von Tiepolo mit seinen Fresken zu europäischer Bedeutung erhoben. Der Name des kostbaren Saales sollte nicht allein an Kaiser Friedrich I. Barbarossa erinnern, der im Mittelpunkt beider Szenen aus der Würzburger Geschichte steht. Es sollte auch dem Kaisertum gehuldigt werden, waren die Bischöfe von Würzburg doch treue Parteigänger der Salier, Staufer und Habsburger gewesen. An das Verhältnis von Staat und Kirche erinnern die vom Domenico Tiepolo gemalten Supraporten:„ Kaiser Justinian legt seine Gesetzessammlung vor“ über der Mitteltür zum Weißen Saal, „Bischof Ambrosius verweigert Kaiser Theodosius den Eintritt in die Kirche“ auf der nördlichen Seite, „Kaiser Konstantin der Große als Beschützer der Kirche“ auf der südlichen Seite.

Gegliedert wird der Kaisersaal durch 20 Dreiviertelsäulen aus Stuckmarmor, die an den Längsseiten weit, an den Schmalseiten eng gestellt sind. In den Nischen der Schmalseiten stehen die außerordentlichen Figuren Neptun und Juno sowie Flora und Apollo des Antonio Bossi. Die großen vergoldeten Wappen der Fürstbischöfe Schönborn und Greiffenclau wurden 1751 nach Formen des Johann Wolfgang van der Auwera gegossen.

Im gleichen Jahr begann Tiepolo mit seinen triumphalen Fresken. Die südliche Schmalseite zeigt die Trauung Friedrich I. Barbarossa mit Beatrix von Burgund, die vor Bischof Gebhard knien, der die Züge Greiffenclaus trägt. Tiepolo, der an keine historischen Vorbilder gebunden war, konnte den Kirchenraum und die Zeugen ganz nach seinem Pathos gestalten. Gegenüber wird in mittelmeerischer Landschaft und vor einem antiken Triumphbogen Bischof Herold, der das Knie beugt, von Friedrich I. Barbarossa mit dem Herzogtum Franken belehnt. Diesmal ist der Kaiser der Gebende, der, von den Statuen des Herkules und der Minerva flankiert, wie ein antiker Herrscher auf dem

Was barocker Jubel in Marmor, Stuck, Gold und Farbe umzusetzen vermochte, offenbart atemberaubend die Hofkirche. Von der Orgelempore aus schweift der Blick zum Marienaltar, wo der Fürstbischof seine Messe las.

The marble, stucco work, gilding and array of color that depict Baroque exultation so well are all breathtakingly combined in the Hofkirche (Court Chapel). This view is from the organ gallery looking towards the Marienaltar where the Prince-Bishop celebrated mass.

La chapelle de la Résidence (Hofkirche) dévoile ce dont le baroque est capable quand il se déchaîne dans les marbres, le stuc, l'or et les couleurs. La vue que nous jetons des orgues sur l'autel de la Vierge, où le prince-évêque disait la messe, nous coupe le souffle.

Marmorthron sitzt. Im Gewölbespiegel führt Apoll die Braut dem kaiserlichen Genius zu, der auf einem prächtigen Thron wartet. Auf einer Wolke rechts vom Sonnenwagen lagern die Fruchtbarkeitsgöttin Ceres, die Liebesgöttin Venus, der geflügelte Amor und Bacchus.

Steht man bei geöffneten Seitentüren nahe den großen Fenstern, dann sieht man nach Norden die Zimmerflucht der Kaiserzimmer entlang bis hin zum grünlackierten Zimmer, einem Höhepunkt des Rokoko. Die südlichen Kaiserzimmer führen von Raum zu Raum zum Spiegelkabinett, das nach langer und aufwendiger Arbeit getreu hergestellt, seit 1987 wieder der Öffentlichkeit zugänglich ist. In seiner leuchtendfrischen Pracht, vervielfältigt durch die Spiegel, findet dieser illusionierende Raum besonders viele Besucher.

Ein letzter Höhepunkt ist die Hofkirche, eingezwängt in ein schmales Rechteck im Südwesten der Residenz, die nur vom südlichen Hofgarten her Licht empfängt. Neumann gelang es, durch eine Längsovalkuppel, flankiert von je zwei Querovalen, die Flächen für lichte Deckenmalereien von Rudolph Byss zu schaffen, die 1945 sehr gelitten haben. Der Musikempore über dem Eingang entspricht über dem Hauptaltar eine Empore mit einem Marienaltar für die tägliche Messe des Fürstbischofs. Gedrehte Marmorsäulen aus Carrara stehen an den Seitenaltären, deren Gemälde von Tiepolos Hand den „Engelsturz“ und die „Himmelfahrt Mariens“ zeigen. Während Antonio Bossi die Stuckfiguren, auch die Kreuzigung am Hauptaltar schuf, gehen die sechs Marmorfiguren auf Johann Wolfgang van der Auvera zurück. Heinrich und Kunigunde am rechten Seitenaltar weisen darauf hin, daß Friedrich Carl auch Bischof von Bamberg war, St. Kilian und Burkard am Hauptaltar erinnern an die Anfänge des Christentums und des Bistums zu Würzburg.

Das Würzburger Mozartfest fasziniert im Juni drei Wochen lang die Besucher. Zum Auftakt am ersten und als Ausklang am letzten Samstag des Festes begeistert die „Kleine Nachtmusik“ Tausende von Zuhörern vor historischer Kulisse.

Würzburg's Mozartfest (Mozart music festival) delights its audiences for three weeks in June with music written by Mozart. The festival begins and ends with an evening concert in the Hofgarten to which thousands flock each year.

La „Mozartfest“ charme pendant trois semaines, au mois de juin, les amateurs de la musique de Mozart. Le Festival débute et se termine un samedi par la «Petite Musique de Nuit» jouée dans les jardins de la Résidence, ce qui attire des milliers de personnes.

The Residence

The Palace of Palaces

There was never a lack of architectural plans for the Residence. Above all, the building was to represent the eternal princely acts of grace, eternal fame and glory. The Residence was not only to provide comfortable living quarters for the Prince-Bishop, in its dimension and appearance it was to proclaim the significance of this spiritual state and the influence of the Schönborn family, then in its third generation of high dignitaries for the Church. In 1719 Balthasar Neumann was contracted to oversee the architectural plans of the Prince-Bishop and coordinate them with his own ideas. Neumann, who remained in charge of the construction until its completion in 1744, had first come to Würzburg in 1711 where he worked in a foundry and with the aid of a stipend from his hometown Eger, took lessons in geometry, surveying and architecture. It is due to the wisdom of the Prince-Bishop that this momentous piece of architecture could be entrusted to the hands of a practically unknown architect whose only claim to fame at the time was three unpretentious terrace houses near the Main River, one of which he resided in himself. There were several interruptions in construction over the years but work was always resumed as the Schönborn family considered the completion of the Residence a matter of prestige.

Neumann succeeded in combining two entirely different palace constructions into one harmonious whole. Each side wing consists of two closed blocks of constructions with two inner courtyards; the two blocks are attached to the main cross lateral section in such a way as to create a Court of Honor of considerable depth. This Court of Honor was cut off from the town by an ornamental iron screen. The screen whose outlines can still be seen in the pavement stones was auctioned off in 1821 in order to draw the town folk closer. In 1894 the Franconia Fountain was erected on the approximate site of the former entrance to the Court of Honor. Below the figure of Franconia, the fountain displays the figures of Walther von der Vogelweide, Germany's most important minnesinger; Tilman Riemenschneider, a renowned local sculpturer; and Mathias Grünewald, a famous late Gothic artist who worked in the region. In order to achieve greater height for his interior, Neumann designed the four storey main facade as two storeys. In the center, three majestic portals enabled a carriage drawn by four horses to enter and leave the vestibule in the appropriate style. The three high windows on the second floor allow light from the setting sun to enter the White Hall. From here a Prince-Bishop could look out onto the Schönborn Chapel where his family lay entombed and in the midst of life be reminded of death – an idea that was not in the least uncommon during the Baroque period. Above the White Hall a Prince-Bishop's coat of arms emblazons while above it is the Imperial crown. The golden Imperial eagle soars atop the blue slate roof. Inside the low, almost squatty vestibule four atlantes bear the weight of the shallow vaulting decorated with the four deeds of Hercules. The vestibule leads to the light and airy Gartensaal and then out to the court gardens. It was here in the Sala Terrena that Prince-Bishops and their courtiers strolled among the freestanding marble columns and contemplated Johannes Zick's splendid ceiling frescos when a hectic schedule did not allow time for a stay at the summer palace in Veitshöchheim. Over Neumann's magnificent staircase is his even more superior unsupported vaulting which was so ingeniously constructed that it even survived the air raids of March 16, 1945. Neumann lived to see Giovanni Battista Tiepolo, the last of the great Venetian fresco painters, "immortalize his name and his art in Germany" by painting the over 600 square meter fresco under the most strenuous conditions: the artist and his sons who assisted him had to paint from a scaffold lying on their backs without really being able to see what was being created as a whole. One does not climb the stairs of the Residence, rather one glides up to the landing, slowly drawing nearer the continent of America colorfully allegorised by an Indian riding an alligator. Turning to ascend the second flight of stairs, one approaches the continent Europe, the land of the arts and sciences, at the foot of which Balthasar Neumann in the uniform of a colonel is seated on a cannon with a whippet beside him. The stucco artist, Antonio Bossi, wearing a heavy yellow cloak, stands somberly to his right. From the lefthand corner wearing his artists's cap, Tiepolo, this huge fresco's master, examines his work with a critical eye. The two doors lead into the White Hall where the eye has a chance to rest before it is required to take in all the grandeur of the Emperor's Hall. Although it was vaulted in 1742, it was not until 1752 after Tiepolo completed his frescos that the Hall became renowned throughout Europe. The name of this room not only pays homage to Emperor Frederick Barbarossa who is depicted twice here, but to the entire concept of the Holy Roman Empire. Tiepolo felt in no way bound to historical exactness. The Green Lacquered Room, the epitome of Rococo, is at the end of the suite of apartments off to the north. The end room off to the south is the Cabinet of Mirrors which was reopened in 1987 after years of extensive work. The Court Chapel, squeezed into the southwest corner of the Residence, again owes its perfection to Neumann's architectural genius. Rectangular in shape on the outside, once inside all spatial sense of direction becomes vague. Five oval vaults – a large longitudinal one in the center flanked on each side by two transverse ovals, galleries decorating the entrance and the front of the chapel, twisted Carrara marble columns adorning the side altars and gilded capitals all blend together to make this a masterpiece of 18C religious architecture.

La Résidence

Château entre les châteaux

La construction de ce château ne put avoir lieu que grâce à un certain Gallus Jakob qui, accusé de détournement de fonds, dut payer la somme énorme de 600 000 florins. Le Prince-évêque Johan Philipp Franz von Schönborn, issu d'une famille de grands bâtisseurs, comme le prouvent les châteaux baroques de Bruchsal et Werneck entre autres, n'avait que l'embarras du choix parmi les architectes célèbres de son époque.

Des courriers spéciaux partaient régulièrement pour Mayence et Vienne d'où les membres de sa famille lui renvoyaient les plans avec des suggestions et des améliorations, bien qu'il ait lui-même une certaine expérience après avoir fait constuire (par Johann Dientzenhofer) le chateau de Weissenstein, près de Pommersfelden, dont les plans avaient été revus par Johann Lukas von Hildenbrandt. La Résidence ne devait pas seulement loger de façon confortable l'évêque et sa cour mais témoigner par sa taille et son aspect extérieur de l'importance et de la richesse de cet état éclésiastique, tout autant qu'elle devait servir à la gloire de la famille des Schönborn. Finalement, ce fut Balthasar Neumann qui fut chargé d'examiner et de coordonner toutes les idées et les plans alors que, jusqu'ici, il n'avait rien réalisé de grandiose; mais il put aller en France prendre les conseils d'éminents architectes. Après la mort du prince-évêque la construction reprit en 1729 avec, cette fois, l'aide de Lucas von Hildebrand et 1737 vit l'achèvement du monumental escalier. Quand en 1740 l'aile des jardins fut terminée, on entreprit immédiatement de décorer les appartements de l'Empereur.

C'est un troisième prince-évêque, Carl Philipp von Greiffenklau, qui réussit à faire venir à Würzburg le dernier plus grand peintre de fresques vénitien: Giovanni Tiepolo qui, accompagné de ses fils, réalisa les fresques de la Salle de l'Empereur et celle de la voûte autoportée qui est le plus grand plafond peint du monde. Elle résista aux bombes et aux flammes qui détruisirent dans la nuit du 16 mars 1945 presque toute la ville et les charpentes du château. Cette œuvre monumentale de 540 m^2 mérite une visite guidée et détaillée. On y voit les allégories des continents connus à l'époque. Nous ne mentionneront que l'Asie vêtue de blanc chevauchant un éléphant, l'Afrique, sous la forme d'une princesse noire, un chameau. L'Amérique symbolisée par une Indienne emplumée fait face à l'Europe, patrie des arts et des sciences. Dans un médaillon le portrait de Carl Philipp von Greiffenklau, entouré de Balthasar Neumann, assis sur un canon, alors que Tiepolo porte son bonnet de peintre et que l'on voit, dans un manteau jaune, Antonio Bossi, le créateur des stucs de la Salle Blanche. Cette salle est éclairée par trois hautes fenêtres donnant à l'ouest sur la chapelle mortuaire des Schönborn, accolée à la cathédrale. Qu'au beau milieu de sa vie Friedrich Carl se voit rappeler sa mort n'a rien d'extraordinaire à l'époque baroque! Cette «Weissen Saal» au décor de rocaille blanche sur fond gris, aux grands lustres de cristal contraste avec la Salle de l'Empereur qui donne sur les jardins. Celle-ci ne porte pas seulement ce nom à cause des fresques montrant le mariage de Frédéric I Barberousse avec Béatrice de Bourgogne, et l'hommage que lui porte l'évêque Hérold recevant le duché de Franconie, mais aussi en l'honneur de tous les Empereurs du Saint Empire Romain Germanique. Des colonnes de marbre, de petits morceaux de miroirs et de remarquables statues de Bossi complètent le décor. En nous approchant des fenêtres nous découvrons une magnifique enfilade de pièces menant au salon vert, au nord et, de l'autre côté, au cabinet des glaces dont la restauration ne fut achevée qu'en 1987. Il reste à admirer la chapelle de la Résidence, elle aussi un pur fleuron baroque.

La vaste place devant le château, (autrefois fermée de splendides grilles de fer forgé de Johann Georg Oegg, qui disparurent en 1821: le dauphin Louis voulant être plus proche de son peuple) est ornée devant la cour d'honneur d'une fontaine offerte en 1894 par la Basse Franconie au Prince Régent Luitpold dont on voit un médaillon sous l'allégorie de la Franconie et, à sa base, des statues des plus grands artistes: Walther von der Vogelweide, Tilman Riemenschneider et du peintre Mathias Grünewald.

Innenstadt

Impression einer Stadt

Als würden die Türme des Doms in Ehrfurcht schweigend die Arbeit von Tilman Riemenschneider betrachten. Unter dem Abendhimmel scheinen sie herüberzublicken zum Fuße des Frankonia-Brunnens.

When Tilman Riemenschneider looks up from his work he sees the towers of the Cathedral reaching up towards the clouds in the sky. The west steeples swing ever so slightly when their 12 bells begin to ring on religious holidays.

Les tours de la cathédrale semblent admirer en silence le travail de Tilman Riemenschneider qu'elles contemplent, au crépuscule, au bas de la fontaine.

Der Dom

Wie ein riesiges Kreuz liegt die Kathedralkirche inmitten der Altstadt. Als Wächter stehen zwei schlanke Türme neben der Westfassade mit dem Hauptportal und zwei jüngere Türme neben dem hochgebauten Chor. Von außen wirkt das mächtige Gotteshaus, sieht man von der barocken Schönbornkapelle ab, wie eine romanische Gottesburg. Im Innern haben die neun Jahrhunderte ihre vielfältigen Spuren hinterlassen, stehen nebeneinander Plastiken der Gotik und Renaissance, barocker Stuck und Schöpfungen unserer Zeit, Zeugen des Glaubens und des Weges der Kirche durch die Epochen.

Der heutige Dom wurde um 1040 von Bischof Bruno, einem Salier, begonnen. Als er 1045 starb, wurde er in der Krypta bestattet, die gleichzeitig mit der Beisetzung geweiht wurde. Erst Bischof Gottfried von Spitzenberg konnte 1188 den Chor des vollendeten Domes weihen. Unter Bischof Hermann von Lobdeburg (†1254) wurde der Chor geschaffen und die Osttürme aufgemauert. Um 1500 bekamen die Seitenschiffe ihre Gestalt mit spätgotischen Fenstern. Erst unter Julius Echter konnte der Italiener Lazaro Augustin 1608 Langhaus, Querschiff und Vierung überwölben. Den gesamten Innenraum stuckierte 1701–1704 der Mailänder Pietro Magno im Geschmack des italienischen Hochbarock aus. Balthasar Neumann schließlich fügte die barocke Schönbornkapelle ans nördliche Querhaus und die beiden Sakristeien an den Chor.

Dieser Dom mit seinen zahlreichen Altären, das Gotteshaus für 30 Generationen, brannte in der Bombennacht des 16. März 1945 aus.

Dem Dom ist im Süden ein gotischer Kreuzgang vorgelagert, der einen „Grashof" umschließt, in dem ein Brunnen zum Grundwasser führt. Über dicht gesetzte Grabplatten führt der Weg. Grabsteine bedecken die Wände des Kreuzgangs.

Gothic cloisters adjoin the south side of the Cathedral. A well out of which ground water can be pumped is located in the middle of the grassy garth. The walk is made up of effigies laid out one next to the other and it leads past even more effigies on the walls of the cloisters.

Un cloître gothique entourant une «cour d'herbe», au milieu de laquelle un puits descend à la nappe d'eau souterraine, se trouve au sud de la cathédrale. Les murs et le sol sont recouverts de pierres tombales en nombre imposant.

Hoch strebt der romanische Chor, den Bischof Bruno über der Krypta aufmauern ließ, flankiert von zwei schlanken Türmen, deren oberste Geschosse der Frühgotik angehören. Die Kuppel der Schönbornkapelle (rechts) steht vor der Kuppel von Neumünster (im Hintergrund).

The high Romanesque choir that Bishop Bruno had raised is flanked by two slender spires whose upper storeys are early Gothic. The dome of the Schönborn Chapel (right) is in the foreground of the Neumünster Church.

Le choeur roman que l'évêque Bruno fit construire au-dessus de la crypte s'élève, flanqué de deux tours minces et élancées dont le haut est déjà en style gothique. La coupole de la chapelle mortuaire des Schönborn à droite devant le dôme de l'église Neumünster.

Da alles Mauerwerk intakt geblieben und der Stuckdekor nur beschädigt worden war, schien ein rascher Aufbau möglich, doch da brach am 20. Februar 1946 die nördliche Hochschiffwand mit den Gewölben über dem Langhaus und dem nördlichen Seitenschiff zusammen und begrub diese Hoffnung. Als 1956 aus statischen Gründen auch die südliche Hochschiffwand neu gebaut werden mußte, verzichtete man auf die Tonnenwölbung und den Stuck im Mittelschiff und setzte eine flache Holzdecke ein, wie sie der romanische Dom besessen hatte. Die Westfassade wurde von den Einbauten des 19. Jahrhunderts befreit, die Westtürme auf ihre ursprüngliche Höhe und Gestalt gestutzt. Erst 1967 war der problemreiche Wiederaufbau abgeschlossen, wurde der Hauptaltar geweiht, wurden als Patrozinium St. Kilian, Kolonat und Totnan eingeführt. Von 1971 – 1975 war das wiedergewonnene Gotteshaus Tagungsort der Synode der Bistümer der Bundesrepublik Deutschland.

Betritt man den Dom durch das Hauptportal, dessen Bronzetüre Fritz König mit der Schöpfungsgeschichte belegte, so steht man vor einem kunstvoll gezierten barocken Gitter. Marx Gattinger hatte es einst für den Abschluß des Chores geschmiedet, um den Bereich des Bischofs und des Domklerus von dem der Pfarrgemeinde abzutrennen, die ihren eigenene Altar am linken Pfeiler der Vierung besaß (1945 verbrannt).

Bevor Sie das Gitter umgehen, sollten sie die Taufkapelle am Ende des rechten Seitenschiffes aufsuchen. Hier halten zwei geknotete, um 1230 gemeißelte Säulen Wache. Sie stammen von der 1644 abgebrochenen Vorhalle und erinnern mit ihren Namen „Booz" und „Jachim" an die ehernen Säulen im Tempel Salomonis in Jerusalem. Unter herabfallendem Licht steht das Taufbecken aus Bronze, das Dompfarrer Walther 1279 von Meister Eckard aus Worms gießen ließ. Dieser bedeutende Bronzeguß des 13. Jahrhunderts schildert mit acht Reliefs Verkündigung, Geburt, Taufe, Kreuzigung, Auferstehung und Himmelfahrt Christi, dazu Pfingsten und das Weltgericht.

Über dem Gitter lastet auf der Empore die Hauptorgel mit 86 Registern. Will man den „heiligen Weg" zum Altar unter der Vierung begehen, so steht man vor einem siebenarmigen Leuchter, den Andreas Moritz, der Künstler, stiftete. Er soll an die sieben Prophezeiungen des Alten Testamentes erinnern, aber auch an die jüdische Gemeinde Würzburgs, die so vielen Verfolgungen ausgesetzt war.

Nun begleitet uns die stolze Reihe der Bischofsgrabmäler, die nur von der im Mainzer Dom übertroffen wird. Sie beginnt mit dem Gedenkstein für Gottfried von Spitzenberg, der 1190 auf dem Kreuzzug starb. Sie endet mit dem Grabmal für Ferdinand von Schlör († 1924). Zu den künstlerisch wichtigsten Werken gehört das Grabmal für Otto von Wolfskeel († 1345) vom „Wolfskeelmeister", dann das 1499 von Riemenschneider für Rudolf von Scherenberg geschaffene Grabmal, das einen unter der Last seiner 95 Jahre gebeugten Greis zeigt, schließlich das Grabmal für Lorenz von Bibra, das dieser Humanist und Gesprächspartner Luthers bereits 1516, drei Jahre vor seinem Tod, in Auftrag gegeben hatte.

In der Vierung steht, von allen Seiten einzusehen, der Zelebrationsaltar, von dem Basler Albert Schilling monumental gestaltet. Sichtbar ruht der Schrein mit den Häuptern Kilians, Kolonats und Totnans, von J. und M. Amberg geschmiedet, im Altar. Zwischen Bischofssitz und Altar wurde das reichverzierte Singepult aufgestellt, das 1644 mit den Wappen des Fürstbischofs Johann Philipp von Schönborn und seiner Domkapitulare belegt wurde. In der Apsis erhebt sich eine Monumentalplastik von Hubert Elsässer: Über der Kathedra stehen die drei Frankenapostel und Patrone des Doms, bekrönt vom apokalyptischen Lamm, darüber, aus einer vergoldeten Scheibe tretend, der wiederkehrende Erlöser, umgeben von den 24 Ältesten, wie es der Evangelist Johannes auf Patmos erschaute. Im Chorschluß zeigt der erneuerte Stuck die Gottesmutter, flankiert von Aposteln, unter der Trinität.

SS·MM·CHILIANO·ET·SOCIIS·PATRIAE·PATRONIS

So schön sieht man selten Würzburgs Pracht. Vor der schieferblauen Kuppel von Neumünster ließ Fürstbischof Johann Philipp Franz von Schönborn die einwärts schwingende Fassade aus rotem Sandstein errichten. Unter seinem Wappen steht Christus Salvator, zur Seite die Bischöfe Kilian und Burkard, auf den Außenpfeilern Kolonat und Totnan.

Prince-Bishop Johann Philipp Franz von Schönborn had the sweeping concave lines of the red sandstone facade built under its slate blue dome. Christ the Saviour stands under the Prince-Bishop's coat of arms; on the sides the bishops Kilian and Burkard and on the outer pillars, Kolonat and Totnan.

Le Prince-Evêque Johann Philipp Franz von Schönborn fit ériger la façade concave de l'église Neumünster dont le grès rouge contraste avec le gris bleu de l'ardoise du dôme. Sous ses armes, le Christ Rédempteur avec à ses côtés les évêques Kilian et Burkard, aux piliers d'angle, Kolonat et Totnan.

Im Querhaus hat sich die Stuckdekoration Pietro Magnos am besten erhalten, mit den stützenden Atlanten und schwebenden Cherubinen, mit der goldstrahlenden Glorie im Vierungsgewölbe über den Evangelisten. Zu Seiten des Chorbogens stehen Maria und Johannes, die einst zum Kruzifix Riemenschneiders aufblickten, das 1945 verbrannt ist. Es wurde durch einen Gekreuzigten aus dem 13. Jahrhundert, der auf einem 1983 geschaffenen Kreuzbalken von H. G. Bücker fixiert wurde, ersetzt. Moderne Fassungen erhielten auch die Madonna von 1420 vom Scherenbergtor der Festung in der Apsis des nördlichen Querhauses und der Apostelaltar in der Apsis des südlichen Querhauses, in dessen Baumgebilde Christus Salvator, Petrus und Andreas stehen, die Riemenschneider für Strebepfeiler der Marienkapelle gemeißelt hatte. Rechts davon das von Loy Hering geschaffene Denkmal für Fürstbischof Konrad von Thüngen († 1540), der mit Hilfe des Schwäbischen Bundes 1525 den Bauernaufstand im Hochstift niederwarf.

Neben den Apsisaltären des Querschiffs erreicht man die Krypta. Auf dem Treppenpodest des rechten Zugangs wurde die bewegte Gruppe des Marientodes aufgestellt, um 1450 von einem mittelrheinischen Meister geschaffen. Da die Krypta als Grabstätte der Bischöfe dienen soll, wurde Josef Stangl (†1979) als erster beigesetzt. Mitten im ältesten Teil unterm Chor steht die Tumba von 1257 mit den Reliquien des hl. Bruno. Unter den Fragmenten ist bedeutend ein spätkarolingisches Steinkreuz mit dem Relief eines bärtigen Kopfes, der vielleicht vom ersten Dombau Mitte des 9. Jahrhunderts stammt.

Im Südosteck des Kreuzganges liegt die Sepultur, die Grablege des Domkapitels. Die Halle aus der Mitte des 15. Jahrhunderts besitzt an der Ostseite sieben kleine Kapellen. Dort leuchten jeden Morgen die farbigen Glasgemälde Georg Meistermanns auf, die den Gang des Kirchenjahres darstellen.

Neumünster

Bischof Bernhard baute nach 990, nahe der Grablege Kilians, ein Kirchlein, das sein Nachfolger, Bischof Heinrich, um einen Chor erweiterte, der Johannes d. Ev. geweiht war. Er soll auch der Begründer des bis 1803 existierenden Kollegiatsstiftes gewesen sein. Entscheidend erweitert wurde der Bau durch eine romanische Basilika mit einem Chor von Bischof Adalbero von Lambach, der die Königin Richeza von Polen als Zustifterin gewinnen konnte. Die unter dem Chor liegende Kreuzgruft ist letzte Zuflucht der Andächtigen vor den kunstbeflissenen Betrachtern des Gotteshauses geworden. Von hier beginnen am 20. August die Pilger der Kreuzbruderschaft ihre Wallfahrt auf den Kreuzberg, hierher kehren sie am 24. August zur Schlußandacht zurück, nachdem sie die „Zwiebelkirwe" (Zwiebel-Kirchweih) in der Semmelstraße durchschritten haben.

Die heutige Gestalt erhielt die Kirche 1711–1719. Anstelle des Westchores wurde der mächtige Kuppelbau errichtet, dessen Vorhalle im Westen die Schaufassade aus rotem Sandstein vorgeblendet wurde. Zum

Hauptportal schwingt sich eine doppelläufige Freitreppe aus grauem Muschelkalk empor. Ihr Sockel umfängt den ebenerdigen Zugang zur Kiliansgruft, die nur im Juli, zum Fest des hl. Kilian, geöffnet ist.

Erhalten blieb im Chor der barocke Stuckmarmoraltar der Brüder Dominikus und Johann Baptist Zimmermann mit Maria zwischen den Evangelisten Markus und Johannes. Johann Baptist freskierte auch die „Anbetung Christi" in die Decke des Chores und die „Himmelfahrt Christi" in die des Langhauses. Das Kuppelfresko, „Die triumphierende Kirche", malte Nikolaus Gottfried Stuber.

In einer Nische unter der Rotunde umfängt Christus mit seinen durchbohrten, vom Kreuz gelösten Armen die Seele des Gläubigen. Eine weitere Nische birgt eine Sandsteinmadonna Riemenschneiders von 1493. Aus seiner Werkstatt stammt das Grabmal des berühmten Abtes Trithemius († 1516) in der Vorhalle.

Falkenhaus

Würzburgs schönstes Bürgerhaus, das „Haus zum Falken", war bis 1406 das Wohnhaus des Dompfarrers und seit 1612 Gasthaus. Im Dezember 1735 erwarb der „fürnehme Handelsmann" Franz Thomas Meisner das Wohnhaus „Zum Falken" und zeigte dem Oberrat an, „daß er das von ihm erkaufte Brentzersche Haus zur Zier der Stadt sowohl von dem vorderen als hinteren Theile nach und nach erbauen wolle". Er ließ die einheitliche Fassade errichten, die auf Geheiß seiner Witwe 1751 von Stukkateuren aus Oberbayern mit dem zarten Stuck überzogen wurde, der bis heute einen Glanz der Lebensfreude des Rokoko bewahrt. Für diese Zier der Stadt wurde sie zehn Jahre von der Steuer befreit; wer seine Fassade in Stein statt Stuck ausführen ließ, war 15 Jahre steuerfrei. An den Bauherrn erinnert bis heute sein Wappen im Mittelgiebel, das verspielte Putten halten.

Die langgestreckte Fassade wird vom Schmuck der Fensterumrahmungen geprägt. Die durchlaufenden Gesimse beider Geschosse tragen als Zierde Engelsköpfe und jugendliche Masken. In der Mitte des ersten Geschosses schwebt Maria in Stuckwolken, von Engeln bekrönt. Drei geschwungene Zwerchgiebel besetzen, durch reichgeschmückte Fenster getrennt, das Dach. Auf dem Mittelgiebel schwingt sich der vergoldete Falke, Wahrzeichen des Hauses, flatternd auf, von vergoldeten Vasen flankiert. Dieses Juwel des Rokoko entstand in einer Epoche des Friedens und Wohlstands, die 1789 ein jähes Ende fand.

Ein Flügel des Kreuzgangs von Neumünster blieb erhalten und wurde im beschaulichen Lusamgärtchen aufgestellt. Das um 1170/80 entstandene Relief zeigt den thronenden Christus, der das Evangelienbuch hält.

One side of the Neumünster cloisters still remains. The relief dating back to around 1170/80 shows Christ seated on a throne holding the Gospels.

Une aile du cloître de l'église Neumünster est restée intacte. Les reliefs qui datent de 1170-1180 montrent le Christ sur son trône tenant les évangiles. C'est une des vues les plus belles du petit jardin Lusam (Lusamgärtchen).

Eine eindrucksvolle Silhouette über den Dächern der Innenstadt. Dom, Neumünster und im Vordergrund die Marienkapelle.
Im Mai treffen sich auf dem weiten Marktplatz Verbindungsstudenten und Bürger zu einem Frühschoppen.

In the month of May fraternity brothers past and present get together at the Marktplatz (Market Place) in front of the Marienkapelle (Mary's Chapel) for a morning glass of wine: the perfect opportunity for an exchange of ideas and opinions.

Au mois de mai se réunissent sur la vaste place du marché, devant la Marienkapelle, les traditionnelles associations d'étudiants et les habitants de la ville qui, en fin de matinée, boivent leur premier verre de vin. Au premier plan la Marienkapelle, derrière elle la cathédrale et l'église Neumünster se détachant sur l'imposante silhouette des toits de la ville.

Marienkapelle

Der „Schwarze Tod", die Beulenpest, war 1346 unter den Krimtataren ausgebrochen und im Jahr darauf von Matrosen in Italien eingeschleppt worden. Von dort verbreitete sich die bösartige Krankheit entlang der Handelsstraßen nach Frankreich und Deutschland. Mißernten begünstigten die Pest, weil die Überträger (Mäuse, Ratten, Flöhe) in die Städte gedrängt wurden. Als sie 1348 den Rhein abwärts wütete, nahmen einige sie als „Strafe Gottes" an, viele jedoch suchten Schuldige und fanden sie in den Juden, die verdächtigt wurden, die Brunnen vergiftet zu haben.

Den Würzburgern war schon lange unheimlich, daß bei Epidemien Juden weniger zu leiden hatten als Christen, was man nicht der besseren Hygiene zuschrieb und der Kunst ihrer Ärzte, sondern der hinterhältigen Vergiftung der Christen. Der Judenhaß war vor allem unter Handwerkern und kleinen Kaufleuten verbreitet, die bei Juden Geld zu hohen Zinsen geliehen hatten. Belegten Bischof und Rat die Juden mit neuen Abgaben, wurden diese auf die Kreditkosten abgewälzt, was die Schuldner erneut erbitterte. Am 21. April 1349 ging das Judenviertel, das sich von der Schustergasse zum Marienplatz hinüberzog, in Flammen auf. Genau wie in Worms und Speyer blieben die christlichen Nachbarhäuser verschont, verbrannten mit den Gläubigern auch die Zeugen und Schuldscheine.

Wie in Bamberg und Nürnberg verschenkte Kaiser Karl IV. die herrenlose Brandstätte zum Bau einer Kirche. In Würzburg ließ Bischof Albrecht von Hohenlohe eine kleine, Maria geweihte Kapelle anstelle der zerstörten Synagoge bauen. 1377 begann auf Veranlassung des Bischofs Gerhard von Schwarzburg die Bürgerschaft mit dem Bau der heutigen Kirche. Dies geschah nicht als Sühne für Brand und Mord im Jahr 1349, es sollte der „unreine“ Platz durch eine Marienkirche entsühnt werden. Der Bau kam nur langsam voran, mußte er doch durch Opfergaben finanziert werden. Zwar war der Chor 1393 vollendet, doch das Langhaus erst 1441, in dessen Nischen der Außenwand zuvor 12 Kramläden gezogen waren. Eberhard Friedeberger aus Frankfurt kann erst 1479 die Spitze auf den Turm setzen lassen. Als 1711 ein Blitz in den Turm schlägt, bekommt er einen barocken Aufsatz mit der Doppelfigur der Immaculata des Jacob van der Auvera. Sie blieb auch an der Spitze des neugotischen Turms, der 1856/57 nach dem Vorbild der Eßlinger Frauenkirche auf stolze 72 Meter erhöht wurde.

Unter den reich geschmückten Portalen ist das um 1420 errichtete Westportal das älteste. Am Mittelpfosten steht unter dem Maßwerkbaldachin die Kopie der Marienstatue eines rheinischen Meisters. Im Tympanon darüber ist das Letzte Gericht dargestellt. Christus verweist als Weltenrichter in den Höllenrachen auch einen König und Bischof. Das Südportal zum Grünen Markt hin trägt im Tympanon die Krönung Mariens, flankiert von der hl. Barbara und Katharina. Die Pfeiler tragen Tilmann Riemenschneiders berühmte Figuren von Adam und Eva in Kopie (Originale im Mainfränkischen Museum). Im Auftrag des Rates der Stadt schuf er 1493 die meisterliche Darstellung des Urelternpaares, wobei er durchsetzte, daß Adam entgegen der Gewohnheit ohne Bart dargestellt

Am oberen Markt, wo das stuckverzierte Falkenhaus an die gotische Marienkapelle stößt, genießen Städter und Besucher bei schönem Wetter das Leben im Freien. Ein Hauch südlichen Flairs liegt dann über der Altstadt.

Local residents and tourists alike gather at the Oberen Markt (Upper Market Place) where the stucco facade of the Falkenhaus (House to the Falcon) stands in sharp contrast to the Gothic Marienkapelle. The atmosphere in the Old Town resembles that of a Mediterranean country.

En haut de la place du marché (Oberen Markt), là où la façade décorée de stuc de la maison au faucon (Falkenhaus) se heurte au style gothique de la Marienkapelle, les habitants de la ville et les touristes profitent des joies de la vie en plein air. Il flotte alors sur la ville un léger parfum de ville méridionale.

MALSOVIT
Lord Extra
Lord Extra
Lord Extra
CAFE WEI
CAFE
Cafe Michel
Konditorei
Bäckerei
Pralinen
Cafe

wurde. Beide verkörpern die vollkommene Schönheit im Sinne der Spätgotik. Das Tympanon des Nordportals trägt eine seltene Darstellung der Verkündigung. Gottvater läßt Christus durch ein Sprachrohr zum Ohr Mariens gleiten. Der Engel der Verkündigung spricht über eine dreisprossige Lilie, Zeichen der Dreifaltigkeit, hinweg zur begnadeten Jungfrau.

Die in den Nischen der Strebepfeiler stehenden Plastiken der zwölf Apostel, Johannes des Täufers und Christus Salvator sind Steingüsse nach den Originalen, die Riemenschneider und seine Werkstatt 1500–1506 geschaffen haben. Von den Originalen ist Jakobus d. Ä. verschollen, stehen Christus, Petrus, Andreas und Johannes der Evangelist im Dom, die anderen im Mainfränkischen Museum. Original ist das Grabdenkmal Riemenschneiders für den Ritter und bischöflichen Marschall Konrad von Schaumberg, der 1499 auf der Heimfahrt vom Heiligen Land auf dem Mittelmeer starb. Der Rat der Stadt vergab als sein Testamentsvollstrecker den Auftrag an Riemenschneider, der den Toten als einen der „letzten Ritter" idealisierte.

Unter den wenigen Grabmälern, die erhalten blieben, fällt das für Martin von Seinsheim (†1434) auf, weil er den Orden der Fürspänger trägt, die in der Marienkapelle ihre Gottesdienste hielten. Dem Orden gehörte auch Ritter Jörg Schrimpf (†1556) an, dessen Grabdenkmal an der Nordseite neben der Silberbüste des aus Würzburg stammenden St. Aquilin steht. An der Südwand lehnt, vom Rauch zahlloser Kerzen geschwärzt, die „Madonna von der Goldenen Pforte" (Westportal), eine hervorragende mittelrheinische Arbeit, um 1440 aus Friedebergers Bauhütte hervorgegangen. Daneben sind in die Wand eingelassen ein Marientod, eine oberrheinische Arbeit, und Christi Kreuzigung am Lebensbaum vom Hohenlohemeister, beide um 1400 entstanden.

Hinter der angestrahlten Marienkapelle, vor dem erleuchteten Falkenhaus wird an Weihnachten in Buden angeboten, was fürs Fest geeignet ist: wohlriechende Gewürze und Lebkuchen, glitzernder Christbaumschmuck, Keramik, Kunsthandwerk und vieles mehr.

Christmas booths in front of the illuminated Falkenhaus have the perfect gift idea: fragrant spices and Lebkuchen, glittering Christmastree ornaments and ceramics.

Devant la maison au faucon brillamment illuminée, on trouve avant Noël tout ce dont on a besoin pour la Fête: des épices odorantes et les gâteaux traditionnels «Lebkuchen», des boules rutilantes et toutes sortes de décorations pour le sapin, des objets en céramique, etc...

Das Juliusspital

Als Julius Echter 1573 Fürstbischof wurde, hatte Würzburg gerade ein Jahr mit Epidemien und einer Hungersnot hinter sich. Da die kleinen Spitäler der Stadt dem Ansturm der Patienten nicht gewachsen waren, starben Menschen hilflos auf der Straße. 1576 begründete er daher ein modernes Krankenhaus und Altenheim, in dem sich Priester, Ärzte und Krankenpfleger um die „unvermögenden und schadhaften Leute" kümmerten, wie es der „steinerne Stiftungsbrief" im Durchgang zum Garten zeigt. Bis zur Säkularisation nahm die Stiftung, die mit Weinbergen, Wäldern und Feldern reich bedacht wurde, auch Pilger für drei Tage auf. Arme, aber begabte Gymnasiasten und Studenten sowie Waisenkinder versorgte man in einem „Musäum". Das Juliusspital mußte für sie Lehr- und Dienstbotenstellen suchen. Um unabhängiger zu werden, besaß das Spital eine Mühle, Bäckerei und Apotheke, bildete eine eigene Pfarrei, deren Pfarrer dem Oberpflegamt angehörte, einem Dreierkollegium, zu dem auch einer der Chefärzte und der rechtskundige Direktor zählten.

Nach Plänen von Georg Robijn war eine große rechteckige Anlage errichtet worden, deren Südflügel an der Juliuspromenade 200 Meter lang ist. Der „Fürstenbau", der ebenso lange Nordflügel, wurde nach einem Brand nach Plänen von Antonio Petrini von Joseph Greising 1704 vollendet. Auf den Giebelschenkeln lagern die Figuren der Barmherzigkeit und Gerechtigkeit, zur Gartenseite die der Frömmigkeit und Religion. Während die Kirche 1945 mit dem ganzen Spital ausbrannte, blieb unter den Arkaden die im späten Rokoko ausgestattete Apotheke erhalten.
Im Garten plätschert ein Brunnen, dessen Flußgötter, Delphine und den krönenden Greif 1706 Jacob van der Auwera schuf. Der von Joseph Greising erbaute Pavillon diente lange als Anatomie, an dem so berühmte Ärzte wie C. C. von Siebold, A. von Koelliker und Rudolf Virchow gewirkt haben.

Den Flüssebrunnen im Garten des Juliusspitals besetzt ein Greif, das Wappentier des Fürstbischofs Johann Philipp von Greiffenclau, der den „Fürstenbau" errichten ließ. Der Pavillon (rechtes Bild) von Joseph Greising begrenzt den Garten im Osten.

An eagle takes flight from the top of the Flüssebrunnen (River Fountain) in the garden of the Juliusspital. It is the heraldic symbol of the Prince-Bishop Johann Philipp von Greifenclau who had the „Fürstenbau" (princely building) erected. The pavilion (right picture) closes off the garden to the east.

Dans les jardins de l'hospice «Juliusspital», l'emblème héraldique du prince-évêque Johann Philipp von Greifenclau, le griffon, (Greif) s'élève de la fontaine. C'est ce prince qui fit construire le «Fürstenbau». A l'est, les jardins sont clôts par le pavillon de Joseph Greising (photo de droite).

Die Alte Universität

Julius Echter, der selbst acht Jahre an fünf außerdeutschen Universitäten studiert hatte, fürchtete, daß die Absolventen des 1561 in Würzburg errichteten Gymnasiums auf fremden Universitäten dem Glauben oder seinem Land verlorengingen. Um die künftigen Priester, Ärzte und rechtskundigen Beamten des Hochstifts im Geiste der Gegenreformation zu bilden, eröffnete er 1582 eine Universität, für die er kaiserliche und päpstliche Privilegien erwirkt hatte. Zum Stiftungsvermögen gehörten auch die Klöster Mariaburghausen bei Haßfurt und Hausen bei Bad Kissingen.

Bauplatz war das ehemalige Ulrichskloster samt anstoßender Häuslein, auf dem der aus dem flandrischen Ypern stammende Mainzer Baumeister Georg Robijn die erste deutsche Universität nach einheitlichem Plan errichtete. Um einen Innenhof baute er drei Flügel, in denen die vier Fakultäten unterkamen, wobei Theologen und Philosophen von Jesuiten unterrichtet wurden, die im anstoßenden Jesuitenkolleg (heute Priesterseminar) wohnten.

An die Südflanke ließ Echter die prächtige Studienkirche (Neubaukirche) stellen, die Professoren und Studenten zum täglichen Gottesdienst aufnehmen sollte. Während die

Der Mittelteil des „Fürstenbaus" des Juliusspitals wirkt wie ein Schloß (links). – Aus Brand und Zerstörung konnte die Apotheke des Spitals im reinsten Rokoko gerettet werden. Um die oft komplizierten Rezepte auszuführen, benötigte ein Apotheker vor 200 Jahren mitunter einen Tag.

The central portion of the „Fürstenbau" of the Juliusspital (hospital) resembles a palace. – The Juliusspital's pharmacy, decorated in the purest Rococo style, has survived fires and destruction. Two hundred years ago a pharmacist needed up to an entire day to fill the somewhat complicated prescriptions.

La partie centrale du «Fürstenbau» semble faire partie d'un château. L'intérieur rococo de la pharmacie de l'hospice a pu échapper aux incendies et à la destruction. Il y a 200 ans l'apothicaire avait parfois besoin de toute une journée pour réaliser les potions prescrites par des ordonnances souvent compliquées.

Flor. Aurantii
Flor. Chamomill. Rom
Flor. Chamomill. vulg
Flor. Chamomill. vulg
Gemmae Populi
Herb. Absynthii
Spec. lignor.
Spec. pectorales

dreischiffige Halle mit ihren zwei Emporen ganz im Stil des Renaissance gehalten ist, zeigen die Fenster zu Hof und Straße gotisches Maßwerk, Erinnerung an eine Zeit, da es noch keine Glaubensspaltung gab. An der Westfassade erhebt sich, von Antonio Petrini auf einem älteren Sockel 1696 begonnen, Würzburgs höchster Kirchturm (79 Meter). Heute dient die einstige Kirche als Aula der Universität.

Rathaus

An das alte Gericht unter einer Linde erinnert der 1597 erstmals aufgemalte grüne Baum, hinter dem der alte Ratssaal liegt, der seit dem Aufenthalt König Wenzels 1397 nach ihm benannt ist. Der Turm wurde 1453 auf seine jetzige Höhe von über 55 Meter hochgemauert und bald darauf vom Uhrmacher Klein mit der ersten öffentlichen Uhr Würzburgs geschmückt. Dort war die Brandwache einquartiert, die bei Feuersbrunst und Feindesnahen die Bürger mit Sturmgeläute zu Hilfe rief.

An der Langgasse lag die Ratskapelle St. Felix und Adauctus (heute Teil des Ratskellers), die einen eigenen Geistlichen, meist einen Ratsherrnsohn, besaß. Westlich vom „Grünbaum" nahm der „Rote Bau", 1669/70 errichtet, den neuen Ratssaal auf,

Die Greisinghäuser (linkes Bild) auf der Neubaustraße sind ein wiedererstandenes Ensemble von Barockhäusern um 1710. – Die Domstraße, einst Marktplatz, ist die belebte Achse der Altstadt geblieben.

The Greisinghäuser in the Neubaustrasse are a reconstructed ensemble of Baroque houses from around 1710. – The Domstrasse, once the market place and center of the Old Town is dominated by the Grafeneckart (left) and the Cathedral.

Les maisons baroques Greising de la photo de gauche (vers 1710) sont un ensemble reconstruit. La rue de la cathédrale (Domstrasse), qui était autrefois la place du marché et l'axe de la vieille ville, est marquée à gauche par l'Hôtel de ville «Grafeneckart» et à l'autre bout par la cathédrale.

Coca-Cola
Coke
Coca-Cola
4 Sanderau
FOTO
OPTIK
Kodak
Duttenhofer

RESTAURANT
WALKÜRE

Hinter dem Kranen, einem Wahrzeichen Würzburgs, das einst den „Commerz" gefördert hat, ragt ein Turm der Pleicher Vorstadt. Den Steinberg begrünen die Weinreben wie ein sanfter Teppich.

A steeple from the Pleich on the outskirts of the city rises behind the Old Crane, a landmark of Würzburg and once the center of trade. Rows of vineyards cover the Steinberg like a velvety green carpet.

Derrière le Crône (Kranen), un emblème de Würzburg, qui favorisa le commerce d'antan s'élève une tour du faubourg Pleich. Sur les hauteurs plantées de vigne du Steinberg, la verdure des ceps semble un moelleux tapis.

während der seit 1985 benutzte neueste Ratssaal im anschließenden, dem Barock nachempfunden Südflügel liegt. Dort erzählt ein riesiges, von Wolfgang Lenz geschaffenes Wandbild von der Geschichte der Stadt. Die einzige Erweiterung gelang 1822 mit dem Ankauf des Klosters der unbeschuhten Karmeliten, einer dreiflügeligen Anlage. In Neurenaissance wurde 1898 noch ein Flügel an der Karmelitenstraße angehängt. 1314 erwarb die damalige Bürgerschaft von Würzburg den „Grafeneckart" für 370 Gulden. Der Turm mit dem angrenzenden Bau hat seinen Namen von einem Vizegrafen Eckart, einem Vertrauten des Bischofs von Querfurt (1201).

Am Alten Kranen

Wenn man von der Alten Mainbrücke zum Steinberg hinüberschaut, fesselt den Blick wohl zuerst der Alte Kranen, der, längst außer Dienst gestellt, eines der Wahrzeichen der Stadt geworden ist. Wer die Festung von Nordosten malen oder fotografieren will, braucht den stämmigen Bau mit den beiden vom Grünspan überzogenen Armen als Gewicht an der linken Seite. Nach einem Entwurf des Franz Ignaz (von) Neumann, Sohn von Balthasar Neumann, wurde er 1772 vollendet.

Zur Mainseite hin zeigt der durch Straßen unterfahrene Bau das Wappen des Fürstbischofs Adam Friedrich von Seinsheim, dem es gelungen war, die zahlreichen Mainzölle bis auf wenige durch Abkommen zu beseitigen und den Warentransport auf dem Main zu beleben.

Nahe der Kranenbastion mit ihrem barocken Wachthäuschen öffnet sich das bescheidene Holztor zur Kärrnersgasse. Es erinnert an Wilhelm von Grumbach zu Rimpar, einen der übelsten Stadtverderber. Um Güter einzutreiben, die ihm Bischof Friedrich von Wirsberg verweigerte, umging er im Morgennebel des 4. Oktober 1563 mit 800 Mann zu Pferd und 500 zu Fuß den Schneidturm, watete am Ufer bis zum Holztor und ließ dort durch mitgeschleppte Zimmerleute die hölzernen Riegel durchsägen. Dann strömten die Soldaten in die Stadt und plünderte sie so, „daß niemand gewesen, der einen Löffel hätte aufheben oder verbergen können". Grumbach, der zwei Domkapitulare als Geiseln genommen hatte, verlangte Ablieferung aller Torschlüssel und Waffen, dazu 10 000 Taler, die nur mit Mühe aufgebracht werden konnten. Wäre die Summe nicht zusammengekommen, hätte er die Stadt in Schutt und Asche gelegt.

Der Blick zum Dom

Auf Balthasar Neumanns Drängen hin wird 1722 der stadtseitige Brückenturm abgerissen, nicht etwa, weil er marode oder verkehrshindernd gewesen wäre, sondern weil er nicht zuließ, daß man vom Scheitel der Brücke ungehindert die Domstraße hinauf und auf die Fassade des Domes blicken konnte. Neumann setzte auch nach zähen Verhandlungen durch, daß die Häuschen an der Brückenauffahrt eingerissen wurden, damit ein repräsentativer Platz vor dem Grafeneckart entstand. Nach der Freilegung wird nach seinen Entwürfen an die Südseite das „Haus zum Hirschen" (heute Dresdner Bank) neu erbaut, wobei der Hirschenwirt zehn Jahre Schatzungsfreiheit erhält, weil er einen „rechtschaffenden" Bau, eines der schönsten Bürgerhäuser Würzburgs, finanziert hatte.

Auf den Platz davor wurde 1733, als die von Neumann projektierte Fließendwasserleitung hier angekommen war, ein Brunnen mit mehreren Röhren aufgestellt. Geschmückt wurde er nur mit einem Schönbornlöwen mit Wappenschild, da Neumann die Summen für einen aufwendigeren Brunnen lieber für die Weiterführung der Wasserleitung eingesetzt sehen wollte. Erst 1761, acht Jahre nach Neumanns Tod, beginnt man den Bau des Brunnens, in dessen vierfach nach außen geschwungenes Becken vier Delphine Wasser speien. Am Fuß des in der Mitte aufragenden schlanken Obelisken stehen die von Lucas Anton van der Auwera entworfenen, von Johann Peter Wagner geschaffenen Figuren der vier Kardinaltugenden (Tapferkeit, Weisheit, Gerechtigkeit, Mäßigung). Obenauf steht, von Wagner gemeißelt, Franconia, die Verkörperung Frankens, mit der Sturmfahne in der Hand. Dieser 1766 vollendete schönste Rokokobrunnen Würzburgs hat am Fischmarkt und auf der Hofstraße jüngere Brüder stehen.

Die Alte Mainbrücke

„Enzelin, der Laie, hat uns eine herrliche Brücke gebaut", ließ Bischof Embricho 1133 in einer Urkunde festhalten. Der Baumeister, der einzige seines Jahrhunderts, der mit Namen genannt wird, muß wohl in den zehn Jahren, in denen die Brücke wuchs, viel gebetet und gebangt haben, denn zu seiner Zeit vermochte man zwar kurze Wölbungen über Kirchenpfeiler zu legen, aber hier waren Spannweiten von 13 bis 17 Meter zu bewältigen. Später, zum Dombaumeister aufgerückt, baute er die Kapelle St. Gertraud in der Vorstadt Pleich, Vorläuferin der heutigen Pfarrkirche. Für seine Zeitgenossen muß die Brücke wie ein Wunder erschienen sein, widerstanden doch die wohlgefugten Steine den Hochwassern, die bis zum Scheitel anstiegen, und den Eisgängen. Zunächst wenigstens, denn das Hochwasser von 1342 und das von 1442 drückte etliche Bogen ein. Es mußten immer wieder Pfeiler erneuert und ausgebessert werden, so daß wohl nur in den flachen und zugebauten Bogen der Brückenrampen noch Steine aus Enzelins Tagen stecken.

Enzelins Brücke säumt der Schmuck barocker Figuren. Fürstbischof Christoph Franz von Hutten, der 1724-29 zwischen den beiden Schönborn-Brüdern regierte, beauftragte 1725 den in Italien geschulten Maler Clemens Lünenschloß, zwölf Figuren zu entwerfen, um die steinernen Buchten über den Pfeilern zu beseelen. Bis zu seinem Tode konnten die Brüder Johann Sebastian und Volkmar Becker für die Südseite sechs Figuren aus gelbem Schilfsandstein schaffen, jede viereinhalb Meter hoch und am Sockel mit dem Monogramm des Fürsten geziert. Dargestellt sind nahe dem Scheitel der Brücke die Immaculata, die Patrona Franconiae, begleitet von den irischen Glaubensboten St. Kilian und St. Totnan zur Stadt hin und St. Kolonat zum Mainviertel hin. Dorthin stellte man die Figuren der im Bistum als heilig verehrten Bischöfe Burkard und Bruno.

Als 1856 in Würzburg die Straßenbeleuchtung eingeführt wurde, glaubte man sich zu allen Nachtzeiten sicher vor Diebstahl, Einbruch und Überfall. Alten Gaslaternen gleichende Leuchten bescheinen den Weg über die Alte Mainbrücke.

When the first street lamps were installed in Würzburg in 1856, the town's citizens felt themselves completely protected against burglary, muggings and street fights. The new street lighting, romantic copies of old gas lanterns, illuminates the walk across the Alte Mainbrücke (Old Bridge).

Quand en 1858 la ville se vit éclairée la nuit, on se crut protégé à toute heure des vols, cambriolages, attaques et bagarres. Les réverbères actuels n'éclairent plus au gaz le chemin de ceux qui empruntent le Vieux Pont sur le Main mais s'efforcent de rendre l'atmosphère du temps jadis.

Im Abendrot sonnt sich die Alte Mainbrücke. Vorne der heilige Kilian, der Überlieferung nach ein irischer Missionar, Maria, die Patrona Franconiae mit dem Sternenkranz und im Hintergrund Kolonat blicken nach Norden, den Main hinunter.

The sun sets on Mary, the Patrona Franconiae, as she looks off to the north. St. Kilian (on the right) and his companion Kolonat (in the background) were both Irish priests who were martyred in 689.

C'est vers le nord que regardent la Vierge Marie, la patronne de la Franconie, à sa droite S Kilian qui mourut martyr en 689 et à gauche son compagnon Kolonat, un prêtre irlandais selon la tradition. Le Vieux Pont (Alte Mainbrücke) dans l'or du soleil couchant.

Als 1729 Friedrich Carl von Schönborn, der Reichsvizekanzler, Fürstbischof wurde, änderte er das Programm seines Vorgängers für die Nordseite. Für dessen Namenspatron Christophorus setzte er St. Nepomuk, den neuen Brückenheiligen ein, für dessen Heiligsprechung 1729 sich das Haus Schönborn sehr eingesetzt hat. An jedem 16. Mai, dem Tag des hl. Nepomuk, erinnern sudetendeutsche Mitbürger mit einem Lichterschwimmen auf dem Main an den Märtyrer des Beichtgeheimnisses. Der Bildhauer Claude Curé hatte die Statuen der Namenspatrone des Fürsten, die Heiligen Fridericus und Carolus Borromäus, auszumeißeln. Der Immaculata wurde der Ziehvater Joseph mit dem Jesusknaben gegenübergestellt.

Aufsehen erregte schon bei den Zeitgenossen, daß als letzte Figur auf der westlichen Seite Karl der Große aufgestellt wurde. Auf Betreiben Friedrich Barbarossas wurde er heilig gesprochen, doch von der Kirche nie anerkannt.

Durch dieses Spalier von Heiligen und Reichsgründern zogen die Habsburger mit großem Gefolge zur Wahl und Krönung nach Frankfurt und dann wieder heimwärts nach Wien.

Inzwischen steht die zweite und dritte Garnitur von Figuren dort, denn die Witterung setzt dem Sandstein arg zu. Für die Erneuerung der Nepomukfigur setzte sich die Ackermanngemeinde ein. Für die Statue Pippins, die am 2. April 1945 in den Main gestoßen wurde, um einem amerikanischen Geschütz Platz zu machen, wurde 1956 Ersatz geschaffen. Um die Baulast an der Brücke entstand dann ein Rechtsstreit, der elf Jahre währte und in letzter Instanz damit endete, daß der Freistaat für die Brücke, die Stadt nur für die Figuren und Gehsteige aufzukommen hat.

Festseelig, wie man hierzulande nun einmal ist, wird seit Juni 1977 ein Brückenfest gefeiert, zur Ehre des über 850 Jahre bestehenden Bauwerks.

Blick nach Westen

Wer der Stadt den Rücken kehrt und auf der Mainbrücke geradeaus blickt, hat ein klassizistisches Tempelchen vor sich, das „Spitäle", einst die Kapelle des Hospitals zu den 14 Nothelfern, das Johann von Allendorf per Testament 1494 für arme Bürger und Bürgerinnen gestiftet hat. Das ausgebrannte Kirchlein dient jetzt als Ausstellungshalle.

Rechter Hand steht bei einem der seltenen Fachwerkhäuser der Stadt im Schmalzhöfchen eine Gedenksäule. Sie erinnert an den hinterlistigen Überfall des Christoph Kretzer am 14. April 1558, der Bischof Melchior Zobel von Guttenberg ermordete, weil er ihm ein Legat von 2000 Gulden verweigerte. Der Bischof verschied auf dem Weg zur Burg, zwei seiner Begleiter blieben tot auf dem Platz.

Hier beginnt der Anstieg der Zeller Straße zur Deutschhauskirche, deren herrliches gotisches Südportal 1288 vollendet wurde. Jahrelang stritt die Bürgerschaft mit dem Deutschen Orden, weil durch die Kirche der öffentliche Weg zum Schottenanger mit der Schottenkirche verbaut werden sollte. Bischof Manigold entschied als Schlichter 1296, daß ein hoher Bogen zwischen Kirche und Turm den Weg freihalten mußte. Nach der Säkularisation völlig ausgeräumt und als Militärdepot verwendet, dient sie seit 1923 einer evangelischen Pfarrei.

Von der Mainbrücke flußaufwärts

Das burgähnliche Gebäude zur Linken der Brücke ist ein 1980 erbautes Kaufhaus, das, hochwassergerecht errichtet, mittelalterlich wirkt. Rechts geht ein Überlaufwehr auf die Schleuse der Rhein-Main-Donau-Schiffahrtsstraße zu, denn der Main ist kanalisiert und soll, sind erst einmal seine zahlreichen Kurven abgeflacht, große Schubverbände vom Schwarzen Meer zum Rhein und von dort zur Donau tragen. Durch die Staustufen träge geworden, wacht er nur manchmal nach Schneeschmelzen mit Dauerregen auf, überflutet die Ufer, drängt in die nahen Gassen und Straßen, die noch nicht durch Hochwassermauern abgeschirmt sind. Die großen Hochwasser sind am Kranen und am Roten Bau des Rathauses in Stein gemeißelt; die letzten, 1970 und 1980 verzeichnet, drangen noch in die Erdgeschosse der Häuser der Büttner- und Kärrnergasse. Menschen, Haustiere und etwas Habe aus den hochwasserbedrohten Häusern zu retten, war Privileg der Fischerzunft, die ihre Gründung auf das Jahr 1020 zurückführt; die älteste erhaltene Urkunde wurde 1279 ausgefertigt. Die Kleinodien der Zunft, der „Silberne Karpfen" und alte Fanggeräte, werden im Historischen Saal der Fischerzunft in der Saalgasse im Sommerhalbjahr ausgestellt.

Oben links segnet Kilian den vorüberschreitenden Betrachter. Das Schwert in der Linken, Zeichen des Martyriums, aber auch Symbol weltlicher Macht der Würzburger Bischöfe als Herzöge von Franken. Kilian ist eine von zwölf monumentalen Statuen, die das Geländer der Alten Mainbrücke säumen.

In his left hand the Apostle Kilian holds a sword, the symbol of martyrdom but also the symbol of the worldly power of the bishops in Würzburg as royal dukes of Franconia. His right arm is extended in blessing. He is one of the 10 monumental figures on the Alte Mainbrücke (Old Bridge).

En haut à gauche de la photo, Kilian, une des statues monumentales du Vieux Pont, élève la main droite pour bénir ou pour prêter serment. Il tient dans sa main gauche l'épée symbole de son martyre mais aussi des pouvoirs laïcs exercés par les évêques de Würzburg en tant que ducs de Franconie. C'est lui qui apporta la bonne parole.

Diesen Blick vom Schloßberg auf St. Burkard und die anschließende Jugendherberge genießen in der Regel nur die Winzer und Winzerinnen der Staatlichen Hofkellerei.

A view of St. Burkard and the adjoining youth hostel from the Schlossberg is a privilege that is usually enjoyed only by the wine-growers from the state-run Hofkellerei.

Cette vue sur l'église S Burkard et l'auberge de jeunesse attenante est en général réservée aux seuls vignerons des vignobles d'Etat de la Hofkellerei.

St. Burkard

In feierlicher Prozession überführte Bischof Hugo 984 die Reliquien des hl. Burkard aus der Kiliansgruft in die Kirche des Andreasklosters, das Burkard, Würzburgs erster Bischof, am Fuß des Marienberges errichtet hatte. Nachdem Kirche und Kloster, die seitdem seinen Namen tragen, bald darauf abbrannten, baute sie Abt Wilemuth neu auf. Zur Weihe dieser romanischen Basilika kam 1042 als Ehrengast Kaiser Heinrich III. Die schmale dreischiffige Kirche überrascht durch den Stützenwechsel von Pfeilern und Säulen aus rotem Sandstein. Da im Westen der Marienberg aufragt, wurden beide Türme am Ansatz des Chores errichtet. Als Johann von Allendorf 1464 das Kloster in ein Ritterstift umwandelte, wurde dieser Chor samt der Krypta abgebrochen, um die Kirche nach Osten um ein Querhaus und einen hohen Chor im gotischen Stil zu erweitern. Vom Chorbogen hängt ein großes Kreuz, das aus der Werkstatt Riemenschneiders kommen soll. Es wurde, wie das Zunftwappen ausweist, von der Fischerzunft gestiftet, die seit alters im Mainviertel beheimatet ist.

Die adeligen Stiftsherren, die erst 1803 die Kirche der Pfarrei überlassen mußten, hatten 1699 ihre Wappen über das Chorgestühl malen lassen. Die beiden barocken Steitenaltäre im Querhaus sind großzügige Stiftungen. Auf dem südlichen, von Franz Rudolf von Hettersdorf gestifteten Altar steht sein Namenspatron Rudolf von Habsburg, dessen Schild die Buchstabenfolge A E I O U trägt. Man hat sie als „Austria Est In Orbe Ultima" (Österreich ist das Äußerste in der Welt) gedeutet. An der Südwand nebenan steht der einstige Pfarraltar, ein Flügelaltar in Renaissanceformen, der Tod, Himmelfahrt und Krönung Mariens erzählt. Die geöffneten Flügel zeigen vier Szenen aus dem Marienleben, geschlossen jedoch Stationen aus dem Leiden Christi. Daneben kann man eine bedeutende Arbeit Riemenschneiders bewundern, eine um 1490 geschnitzte und fein gefaßte Büste der hl. Maria mit dem sitzenden Jesuskind.

Hermann Hesse beschrieb sie: „Eine traurig schöne Madonna mit langen Augenlidern und dünnen Prinzessinhänden. Traumhaft blickt sie aus ihrem Glasgehäuse hervor, unserer Welt fern, einer anderen Welt und Luft bedürftig, die man ersatzweise durch das dünne Glasgehäuse zu leihen versucht hat, in der Anmut und Vornehmheit ihrer Trauer weit über uns heutige Menschen hinaus verfeinert."

Anmutig und fein sind auch die Reliefs aus einem Würfelkapitell des ausgehenden 13. Jahrhunderts, das als Opferstock an den Treppen von der romanischen Kirche zum gotischen Querhaus dient. Vier Szenen füllen die Schilde: Christus erscheint Magdalena als Gärtner; Christi Himmelfahrt; die Madonna thront zwischen zwei Engeln; die hl. Dreifaltigkeit. Nur eine Generation jünger ist das Kreuzigungsrelief nahe dem nördlichen Ausgang, das erst 1881 in die Kirche geholt wurde, von einem Ehepaar Brunlin für das Leprosenhaus vor dem Zeller Tor gestiftet. Unter dem Kreuz mit der in Ohnmacht sinkenden Maria und dem von tiefem Schmerz gepeinigten Apostel Johannes erweckt ein Löwe durch Anhauchen seine Jungen. In der Bekrönung reißt sich über zwei Propheten ein Pelikan die Brust auf. Die Auslegung sagt, daß nur der vom Atem des Hl. Geistes berührte Mensch zum echten Leben erwacht, daß Christus sein Blut für die Erlösung der Menschen hingegeben habe, wie der Pelikan seines für seine hungernden Jungen.

Verläßt man St. Burkard durch diesen Ausgang, hat man linker Hand die Vorhalle mit hohen Rundbogen. In der spätgotischen Spitzbogennische wurde 1511 ein Ölberg aufgebaut, der in unserer Zeit durch eine Kopie ersetzt wurde.

Das Käppele

Um 1640 trug der Sohn eines Fischers aus dem Mainviertel ein geschnitztes Vesperbild auf den Kleßberg (Nikolausberg) und stellte es auf einen Bildstock. Bald schützte ein schlichtes Häuschen das Bild der trauernden Mutter Maria mit dem Leichnam ihres Sohnes auf dem Schoß. Schäfer, die ihre Herden auf dem kahlen Kopf des Berges hüteten, Häcker, die ihre Weinberge an der Ost- und Südflanke bearbeiteten, verweilten im Gebet vor dem Bild. Da erste Wallfahrten aus der Stadt einsetzten, ließ Fürstbischof Johann Philipp von Schönborn durch seinen Weihbischof alle Aussagen über Gnadenerweise protokollieren. Da berichtete etwa die Frau eines Häckers, sie habe, taub geworden, sich mit einem wächsernen Kopf zum Bildhäuschen verlobt; geheilt, habe sie, mit drei anderen Frauen, ein neues Häuslein errichten lassen.

Da immer mehr Hilfesuchende den Berg heraufpilgerten, vor allem zum Pfingstfest, auch fleißig in die Opferstöcke gaben, wurde der Pfarrer von St. Burkard beauftragt, eine Kapelle („Käppele“) bauen zu lassen, die 1684 vollendet war. Als Johann Gottfried von Guttenberg 1684 Fürstbischof wurde, förderte er zwar tatkräftig die Wallfahrten nach Mariabuchen, Dettelbach und Fährbrück, lehnte aber die zum Käppele ab, weil es schon zu viele gebe und die Wallfahrt nach Höchberg darunter litte. Da erschienen aber rechtzeitig Wunderzeichen, die das Käppele ins rechte Licht rückten. So hörten etwa Wachtposten und Offiziere um vier Uhr früh ein Glöckchen läuten, die Schloßwache sah gar die Kapelle in Brand stehen, andere sahen brennende Fackeln den Berg hinabziehen. Der Fürstbischof zog seine Bedenken zurück.

Als der Andrang zunahm, vor allem an den Festen Mariä Schmerz (15. September) und Mariä Heimsuchung (31. Mai, damals 2. Juli), wurde die Kapelle aus Spenden 1713 erweitert, 1741 um ein offenes Kapellchen ergänzt, an dem für die eine Messe gelesen werden konnte, die im Innern keinen Platz hatten finden können. 1747 wurde die Seelsorge den Kapuzinern übertragen, die in ihrem schlichten Kloster neben der Kirche bis heute für Gottesdienst und Pilgerpredigt sorgen.

Im gleichen Jahr setzte Fürstbischof Anselm Franz von Ingelheim Pfleger für die zahlreichen Stiftungen und Opfergelder ein, um eine Kirche neben die Gnadenkapelle zu bauen, für die Balthasar Neumann schon 1736 Pläne ausgearbeitet hatte. Er errichtete einen nach Süden gerichteten Zentralbau. An den quadratischen Mittelraum mit den abgeschrägten Ecken legt sich nach Süden der Chor, nach West und Ost Kapellen. Die nach Osten ist geöffnet zur alten Gnadenkapelle, die erst 1778 aufgemauert und mit einer Kuppel überdacht wurde. Nach Norden ist eine Vorhalle mit der Orgelempore vorgelagert. An deren Ecken stehen die Türme, die schlanke Kuppeln mit goldenen Kreuzen tragen. Reich gegliedert ist nur die Nordfassade zwischen den Türmen. Über dem Portal steht in einer Nische, von Johann Peter Wagner geschaffen, die Figur Mariens.

Seit 1761 gelangen Wallfahrer wie Besucher zur Kirche über eine doppelläufige Treppe, an der mächtige Platanen stehen, die weithin den Kreuzweg markieren. In den Kapellen auf den einzelnen Terrassen stehen figurenreich die 14 Kreuzwegstationen, die Johann Peter Wagner schon in der Manier des Rokoko schuf. Vor jeder Kapelle bis hin zum hl. Grab sprachen die Walleut die vorgeschriebenen Gebete, rückten auf den Treppen nach einem Vater Unser und einem Ave Maria eine Stufe weiter, bis die letzte Terrasse erreicht war. In der Gnadenkapelle unter dem Deckengemälde, das Matthäus Günther 1781 malte – es zeigt die Himmelskönigin, umgeben von der Geschichte Judiths –, singen und beten die Gläubigen vor dem Gnadenbild, das im Glasschrein auf dem Hauptaltar steht. Seit 1797 besitzt das Käppele ein zweites Gnadenbild, eine spätgotische Madonna mit Kind aus dem Domkreuzgang, die zuvor auf der Vogelsburg bei Volkach stand. Wer Heilung suchte, wer Heilung fand, erinnerte mit

In winterlicher Landschaft schweift der Blick über den Main. Von den Villen der Mergentheimer Straße zum schloßähnlichen Haus der Burschenschaft Germania. Dahinter zieht der Kreuzweg den Berg hinauf zum Käppele.

A winter setting. The eye wanders from the villas in the Mergentheimer Strasse upwards to the castle – like fraternity house Germania behind which the stations of the cross ascend to the Käppele (Small Chapel).

Les stations du chemin de croix menant à la Käppele sur la colline Nicolas (Nikolausberg) vont de terrasse en terrasse, la première est cachée par la maison des étudiants: (Burschenschaft) Germania.

einem Wachsgeschenk daran. Heute, da man sich gegen alle Gefahren, auch gegen Sonnenbrand im Urlaub, versichern kann, mag man darüber lächeln oder den Kopf schütteln. In einer Zeit, da man wehrlos war gegen die Unzahl von Krankheiten, wo Hunger und Armut die Menschen anfällig machten, da war Maria die große Zuflucht. Die Kapuziner haben den Mirakelgang inzwischen etwas gelichtet.

Tritt man von der schlichten und etwas dämmerigen Gnadenkapelle hinüber in Neumanns Kirche, läßt das Licht aus der Kuppel und den Chorfenstern den Hochaltar aufleuchten. Das Gemälde in der Kuppel, 1752 von Matthäus Günther freskiert, schildert die Herrlichkeit Mariens im Himmel und ihr Wirken als Patronin Frankens. In den Querarmen wird an Vorbilder Mariens aus dem Alten Testament erinnert: Abigail, die David besänftigt, Esther, die vor Ahasver um ihr Volk bittet. Im Chor wird die Anerkennung der Wallfahrt durch Fürstbischof Johann Philipp, über der Orgel die Genehmigung des Neubaus durch Fürstbischof Anselm Franz festgehalten. Die kleineren Bilder schildern wunderbare Begebenheiten aus der Geschichte der Wallfahrt. Die gleichzeitigen Stukkaturen, großzügiges Muschelwerk mit zahlreichen vorzüglichen Putten, schuf der Wessobrunner Johann Michael Feichtmayr.

Neumann erlebte noch die herrliche „Auszierung“ der Kirche, nicht mehr den von ihm geplanten Stationsweg, auch nicht die Weihe der Altäre. Erst 1768 waren wieder so viel Opfergaben zusammengekommen, daß die Seitenaltäre aufgestellt werden konnten. Für den linken Altar malte Johannes Zick die Marter des hl. Vitus, für den rechten Nikolaus Treu den hl. Nikolaus, der einen losgekauften Sklaven segnet. Den Hochaltar konnte Georg Winterstein erst 1799 als klassizistische Baldachinanlage vollenden. Das Altarblatt stellt die Heimsuchung Mariens dar, sehr wahrscheinlich von Konrad Huber gemalt, der auch die Gemälde der Altäre der Gnadenkapelle geliefert hatte.

Wenn im Sommer der erste Gottesdienst des Sonntags zelebriert wird, wenn in der Maiandacht zu brausender Orgel Marienlieder erklingen, wenn die aufgesteckten Kerzen sachte flackern, dann begreift man etwas von der starken Verwurzelung Mariens in „ihrem Herzogtum“.

Von Terrasse zu Terrasse steigen die Kapellchen mit den Kreuzwegstationen empor zum Käppele auf dem Nikolausberg. Vierzehn bewegte Passionsszenen von Johann Peter Wagner geleiten den nachdenklichen Besucher zur Marien-Wallfahrtskirche.

The stations of the cross ascend from terrace to terrace to the Käppele on the Nikolasberg. The sculpturer, Johann Peter Wagner, was well-known not only for his putti angels but also for his moving interpretation of Christ's path to the Cross.

Le chemin de croix qui monte à la chapelle de la Käppele fournit la preuve que Johann Peter Wagner ne savait pas seulement faire de petits amours baroques mais aussi ces quatorze impressionnantes scènes de la Passion du Christ.

Ins Licht der Scheinwerfer getaucht, tritt das Käppele aus dem Dunkel der Nacht.

Immersed in floodlights, the Käppele as well as the fortress Marienberg on the next hill stand out from the dark of the night.

Illuminée par des projecteurs, la Käppele se dresse dans la nuit, tout comme la forteresse sur la colline voisine.

Grüne Lungen für Berg und Tal

Nicht nur der Nikolausberg war kahl, alle Berge um Würzburg sammelten die Sommerhitze und strahlten sie ab, in die Weinberge und in die Stadt. Nicht nur Caroline Schelling, deren Gemahl von 1804 bis 1806 seine Philosophie in der Universität vortrug, stöhnte unter der Hitze und monierte die fehlenden Wälder. Auch Felix Dahn, Professor der Rechte und Verfasser des vielgelesenen Romans „Ein Kampf um Rom“, der eigens vor die Stadt gezogen war, um bessere Luft zu atmen, litt unter der Hitze, wurde aber von den Einheimischen belehrt, daß, wer einen guten Wein trinken wolle, eben auch ertragen müsse, daß die Trauben „gekocht“ würden.

Nun wuchsen auf den Kuppen der Berge gar keine Reben. Dort weideten Schafe das Gras ab, wurden Kalksteine gebrochen, auf dem Nikolausberg für eine Kalkbrennerei, da der Bruch keine tauglichen Hausteine hergab. Während des deutschfranzösischen Krieges faßten einige Bürger, die dann 1874 den Verschönerungsverein gründeten, den Plan, den Nikolausberg zu begrünen. Man wollte heraus aus der Stadt, deren Befestigungsmauern eben abgetragen wurden, deren Ringparkanlagen erst entstanden, um sich bewußt „der Naturschönheiten mit Muße und Bequemlichkeit erfreuen zu können“. Der Vereinsgründer, Notar Johann Michael Seuffert, konnte einleuchtende Gründe für die Anpflanzungen anführen:„ Derartige Einrichtungen würden jedermann Veranlassung geben, öfters ins Freie zu gehen und sich kräftigende Bewegung zu machen, insbesondere aber die reinere Luft der Anhöhen zu atmen!“

Als die Aufforstung der Kuppe gelungen war, wurde aus Spenden von Vereinen und der Bevölkerung die Frankenwarte erbaut, ein Aussichtsturm, von dessen Kanzel man bis zu den Rändern des Spessarts, der Rhön und des Steigerwalds sehen konnte. Auf dem Steinberg war schon 1876 eine Allee aus Walnuß- und Zierbäumen angelegt worden als Rückgrat einer Aufforstung mit Birken und Eichen, Weißbuchen, Lärchen und Kiefern. Das Wäldchen wurde bald nach Otto von Bismarck benannt, dem Reichskanzler, der in Würzburg seine Anhänger hatte. Zu seinem 90. Geburtstag 1905 wurde der Bismarcksturm errichtet, an dem gelegentlich nationale Verbände feierten. Auf angekauften Ödungen und Äckern auf der Gerbrunner Höhe wurde bis 1878 das Sieboldswäldchen angelegt, das an den Arzt und Japanforscher Philipp Franz von Siebold erinnern sollte, der zahlreiche japanische Pflanzen eingeführt und akklimatisiert hatte.

Um einen schattigen Weg zum Wald zu erhalten, der bis zur Eingemeindung Heidingsfelds (1930) diesem Städtchen gehörte, wurden Flächen am Nordhang des Dallenberges und im Steinbachtal angekauft. Diese Anlage wurde später ein bevorzugtes Ausflugsziel der Würzburger. Auch hier wurde 1905 ein Denkmal enthüllt, eine von Arthur Schleglmünig geschaffene Bronzeplakette für Friedrich von Schiller zu dessen 100. Todestag. Die Verbindung zur Frankenwarte stellte die 1895 kultivierte Schlucht dar, die der Besitzer V. A. Fischer nach seiner einzigen frühverstorbenen Tochter „Annaschlucht“ benannt hatte.

Der Ringpark

Stand hinter dem Bau der Grünanlagen auf den Höhen und im Steinbachtal ein Verein, engagierter Bürger, so verdankt der Ringpark seine Existenz der Stadt. Sie erreichte nach rund 40 Jahren mit Eingaben und Vorstellungen 1856 die Aufhebung der Festungseigenschaft für die rechtsmainische Stadt und kaufte 1868, zwei Jahre nach dem verlorenen Krieg gegen Preußen, die rechtsmainischen Festungswerke samt dem Glacis, dem freien Schußfeld, das schon Alleen und Baumgruppen besaß. Im Jahr darauf begann man die Festungsmauern sorgfältig abzutragen, um die behauenen Steine verkaufen zu können, ausgenommen die Bastion hinter dem Hofgarten, die als dessen Stützmauer erhalten werden mußte. Den Erdwall hinter der geschleiften Mauer schüttete man in den breiten Graben und bepflanzte das Areal mehr, wie 1. Bürgermeister Georg Zürn anmerkte, „nach natürlichem Geschmack und Schönheitssinn" als nach einem kunstverständigen Plan.

Zum Gestalter der großen Anlage wurde der 1880 zum Stadtgärtner berufene Schwede Lindahl, der den Park zum Kunstwerk entwickeln wollte, was nicht nur Geld, sondern auch manchen Baum kostete, der nicht ins Konzept paßte. Die jahrelangen Angriffe und Vorhaltungen wegen verschwenderischen Umgangs mit Gemeindevermögen, schließlich die Einsetzung einer Prüfungskommission verletzten den sensiblen Mann so, daß er sich in den Anlagen nahe der Ottostraße im November 1887 erschoß. Ein Brunnen und eine Gedenksäule erinnern dort an sein Schicksal.

Hatte man einst der lukrativen Versuchung widerstanden, einen Teil des Parks für eine Ringstraße nach Wiener Muster zu opfern, so gab man vor gut zwanzig Jahren den Forderungen des Verkehrs nach und beschnitt den Ringpark zwischen Friedensbrücke und Berliner Ring. Dort ist er denn auch verödet. Wo man ihn beließ, ist er der beliebte Spazierweg geblieben, dessen Bänke zum Ausruhen und Betrachten einladen.

Viele Bürger und Besucher zieht es von Frühjahr bis Herbst nach Klein-Nizza im Rücken des Hofgartens, zu den bunten Vögeln in ihren Volieren, zum Teich mit den chinesischen Brautenten. Hier und drüben im Hofgarten schlagen in warmen Nächten die Nachtigallen.

Auch der Ringpark erhielt sein Denkmal, den Studentenstein, der in die Wiese vor der Neuen Universität am Sanderring gestellt wurde. Einst sollte er an die im Ersten Weltkrieg gefallenen Studenten erinnern. Nun erinnert der schwere graue Block auch an die akademische Jugend, die im Zweiten Weltkrieg fiel oder hingerichtet wurde, weil sie Widerstand leistete. Ein Mahnmal ist er geworden, einen weiteren, letzten Krieg zu verhindern.

Welchen Eindruck muß das von Stuck und Vergoldung schimmernde Kirchenschiff mit dem kostbaren Tabernakel auf die Wallfahrer gemacht haben, die aus ärmlichen Verhältnissen kamen. Aller Glanz sollte der Ehre Gottes dienen.

What an impression the stucco work and glistening gilding of the nave with its splendid tabernacle must have made on the pilgrims who often came from humble surroundings. All this resplendence was to the glory of God and the Virgin Mary.

Comme les pélerins, souvent issus de milieux simples, pauvres même, devaient être impressionnés par le décor doré et les stucs de la nef menant au tabernacle précieux! Toute pompe à la plus grande gloire de Dieu!

Nur im Winter geben die alten Platanen den Blick vom Käppele den Kreuzgang hinunter frei. Abwärts schreitend führt uns der Leidensweg Christi zum Ursprung seines Opfergangs im Haus des Pilatus.

It is only in the wintertime that the Käppele (Small Chapel) can be seen through the plane trees. Descending Christ's path of Calvary, we are led back to the first station, the house of Pontius Pilot.

Ce n'est qu'en hiver, quand les vieux platanes ont perdu leurs feuilles, qu'on peut voir la forteresse de la Käppele. Le chemin de croix qui descend nous mène à l'origine de celui ci: la maison de Ponce Pilate.

Als der Studentenstein noch nahe der Löwenbrücke stand, konnten die Aktiven des Corps Rhenania ihn vor sich sehen. Das Corps besitzt das Sommerschlößchen, das sich Fürstbischof Christoph Franz von Hutten ans Westende seines Gartens bauen ließ. Als die Auffüllung der Schießhausstraße drohte, wurde das Huttenschlößchen um 90 Grad zum Ringpark hin gewendet, was die „Alten Herrn" 1904 aus eigener Tasche bezahlen mußten. Ein Palais jüngerer Bauart besitzt die Burschenschaft Germania unterhalb des Käppele beim Beginn des Stationsweges. Weitere Verbindungshäuser stehen an der Mergentheimer und an der Rottendorfer Straße.

Die Studenten der 27 Verbindungen waren immer eine Minderheit an der Universität, die 1889 rund 1660 Studenten hatte, heute aber rund 18 000, darunter zahlreiche Studentinnen, deren erste Kommilitonin 1904 zugelassen wurde. Neben der Alten Universität in der Domerschulstraße, die Julius Echter bauen ließ, und der Neuen Universität am Sanderring wird gelehrt und geforscht in den Instituten am Röntgenring und in der Koellikerstraße, in den Kliniken des Luitpoldkrankenhauses und im neuesten Universitätsviertel am Hubland an der Stadtgrenze zu Gerbrunn. Dort steht auch die

Universitätsbibliothek, die neben ihren 1,2 Millionen Bänden auch die in der Säkularisation aus den Stiften und Klöstern weggeholten Handschriften verwahrt. Wertvollster Bestand sind Handschriften aus der einstigen Dombibliothek, deren erstes Verzeichnis um 800 angelegt wurde. Schon Bonifatius und seine Mitarbeiter forderten unermüdlich Bücher aus ihrer angelsächsischen Heimat an, die dann in den Klöstern wie Fulda oder den Domschulen wie Mainz und Würzburg abgeschrieben wurden. Als sich 1631 die Schweden näherten, versteckte man den größten Teil der Dombibliothek auf dem Dachboden des Doms, wo er 1717 von Christoph Franz von Hutten, dem späteren Fürstbischof, wieder aufgefunden wurde.

Im Südflügel der Residenz stellt die Universität nicht nur im Martin-von-Wagner-Museum ihre Kunstgegenstände aus, sie präsentiert dort auch eine einmalige Sammlung griechischer Vasen aus dem 4. vorchristlichen Jahrhundert, die aus etrurischen Gräbern geborgen wurden.

Old Town
Impressions

The Dom (Cathedral)

The Cathedral is laid out like a gigantic cross in the middle of the Old Town whose perimeter has been compared to a miter or a bishop's cap. Two slender towers stand guard on the west main face while two more recently constructed towers flank the high choir. Apart from the Baroque Schönbornkapelle, this overpowering edifice resembles a Romanesque fortified church on the outside. On the inside, the church's 900 year history has left behind manifold traces from Gothic and Renaissance statues to Baroque stucco and 20th century works of art standing side by side. The Cathedral as it stands today was begun around 1040 by Bishop Bruno, who, when he died in 1045, was consecrated and buried in the church's crypt. It was not until 1188 that the choir could be dedicated. Various changes took place throughout the centuries: In the 13th century the choir was vaulted and the east towers raised; around 1500 the side aisles were vaulted and high Gothic windows were put in; under Julius Echter the nave and transcept were also vaulted while from 1701-1704 the entire interior was decorated in stucco; Balthasar Neumann added the Baroque Schönbornkapelle onto the northern transcept and the two sacristies to the choir. This Cathedral with its numerous altars, its exquisite Baroque wrought iron choir gate, its 13th century baptismal font, Neumann's effigies for Rudolf von Scherenberg and Lorenz von Bibra, and Pietro Magno's stuccoed marble altar burned during the bombing of Würzburg on March 16, 1945. The walls, however, remained intact and the stucco work was only damaged. Therefore, plans for a speedy reconstruction seemed possible. Barely a year later though, the north walls of the nave and side aisle caved in and all hope for an immediate start had to be abandoned. In 1956 as the south nave wall had to be rebuilt as well, the vaulted ceiling of the nave was replaced by a flat wooden one like the Romanesque church had had. The 19th century decorations were removed from the west facade and the frontal towers reduced to their original form and height.

Neumünster Church

After 990 Bishop Bernhard had a small church built near Kilian's grave. Bernhard's successor added a choir that was dedicated to the Evangelist John, who is also said to be the founder of the collegiate church that existed here until the secularization in 1803. The church received its present facade, an interplay between Baroque and Rococo, between 1711-19. The west choir was replaced by an immense dome whose vestibule makes up the lovely red sandstone facade and the west entrance. A freestanding double staircase out of grey muschelkalk leads up to the entrance. The street level entrance to St. Kilian's sepulchre, which is only open during the octave of Kilian, is at the base of this staircase.

Marienkapelle

On the night of April 21, 1349, Würzburg's Jewish ghetto (approximately the area which makes up the Market Place today) went up in flames while not a Christian home was touched by the fire. Afterwards a small chapel was erected on the site of the former synagogue and in 1377 Würzburg's inhabitants began with the construction of the Marienkapelle (Mary's Chapel) not because they felt remorse for the lives that had been lost due to the fire, but because the site was to be purified through the erection of a House of God. Construction was slow; the choir was completed in 1393, the nave in 1441 and in 1470 the roof. The first tower was completed even later (1479) and over the centuries it underwent several changes. Jacob van der Auvera created the Baroque Virgin that crowns the present Neo-Gothic spire. All three portals are richly decorated; the west one being the oldest (1420). The columns of the south portal opening onto the market square bear copies of Tilman Riemenschneider's famous Adam and Eve (originals in Mainfränkisches Museum). Adam is depicted without a beard; both are superb examples of the perfection the late Gothic strived to achieve. The tympanon above the north portal is a most unique representation of the Annunciation; the Holy Ghost is the speaking tube that God the Father is speaking through to the Virgin.

Falkenhaus (House to the Falcon)

Würzburg's most superb patrician mansion, the House to the Falcon, was the home of the Cathedral's priest before it became an inn. In the 18th century it was bought by a dignified merchant who wanted to make the building the city's jewel of ornamentation. He had the facade redone in a delicate layer of stucco – the reflected splendor of the light-hearted spirit and exhileration that was so typical of the Rococo. As a sign of appreciation, the city charged no real estate taxes on the edifice for ten years. Playful putti figures hold the merchant's shield in the middle of the gable above which the falcon, after whom the building is named, flaps his wings. The facade's luxuriant window ornamentation with its pilasters and miniature roofs, its shell decorations and putti angels bears evidence of the period of peace and prosperity that it was created in.

The Generosity of Julius Echter

When Julius Echter became Prince-Bishop in 1573, Würzburg had just gone through a year of epidemics and near starvation. The small charitable institutions in the town had more to do than they could handle and consequently, people were dying in the streets. In order to alleviate the problem, Echter had a modern hospital and an old age home built in which priests and doctors could care for the poor and the needy. As this religious charitable institution was richly endowed with vineyards, fields and woodlands, it could also afford to take in pilgrims (for 3 days), gifted students and orphans among others. The institution had its own mill, bakery, pharmacy and its own parish. In order to educate future priests, doctors and various administrators in the spirit of the Counter-Reformation, in 1582 Julius Echter founded a university that enjoyed imperial and papal privileges. A student church, the Neubaukirche, was erected to insure that students and professors would attend mass daily.

Rathaus (Grafeneckart) Town Hall

In 1314 the town council purchased the Grafeneckart from a knight who was heavily in debt. The green tree "Zum Grünen Baum" was first painted on the building in 1597, and is symbolic of the linden tree that once stood on the spot as the law court convened there. The 15th century clock on the 55 meter high tower was the first public clock to be hung on a building. A tower once stood next to the Grafeneckart at the head of the Alte Mainbrücke (Old Main Bridge) but it was ordered torn down in 1722 by Balthasar Neumann not because it was dilapidated or because it impeded traffic but rather because Neumann felt that the view of the Cathedral from the city end of the bridge should remain unobstructed.

Alte Mainbrücke (Old Main Bridge)

"Enzelin, the layman, has built a magnificent bridge for us." These are the words that document the completion of the Old Main Bridge in 1133. During the ten years of construction, Enzelin, the only architect mentioned by name in the 12th century, must surely have spent alot of time praying that the unusually wide 13-17 meter arches would hold. At the time the way the stonework construction withstood flooding and drifts of ice made the bridge seem like a small miracle. Later repairs were necessary, but some of the original stones are still part of the bridge. In the 18th century plans were made for 12 statues to decorate the bays of the piers. Six 4.5 meter high yellow sandstone figures whose lives were closely linked to the history of Würzburg were designed for the south side: The Virgin as the patron saint Franconia accompanied by the Irish-Franconian apostles St. Kilian, St. Totnan and St. Kolonat. Although they were not officially canonized, Burkard, Würzburg's first bishop, and Bruno, an 11th century bishop, were considered holy by the diocese and thus found their places on the bridge as well. St. Nepomuk, for whom the Schönborn family used its influence to have him canonized in 1729, stands next to St. Fridericus and Carolus Borromäus, the patron saints of the bridge's patron. The end figure of Charlemagne aroused some attention as he was never officially recognised by the Church; however, his presence on the bridge is in honor of his founding the Holy Roman Empire which Würzburg's bishopric supported. King Pippin, who in 742 endowed the newly-established bishopric with land and parochial tithes, was the last figure erected. The Habsburger and their entourages nobly passed between these rows of saints and founders of the Empire on their way to imperial elections and coronations in Frankfurt and on their way home to Vienna. The sun shone brightly on the gilded palm leaves of the martyrs, the swords of the bishops and the crowns of the Franconian rulers.

St. Burkard

In 984 Bishop Hugo transferred the relics of St. Burkard from the Kilian sepulcher to the cloister church that Burkard, Würzburg's first bishop, had erected on the southeast slope of the Marienberg. The Romanesque church and cloister burned down a short time later after which a new basilica was begun a bit further to the north. Emperor Heinrich III came as the guest of honor to the dedication of St. Burkard's in 1042. In 1464 the cloister was turned over to a knightly charitable institution and the choir and crypt were torn down in order to expand the church to the east with a transcept and a Gothic polygonal choir. St. Burkard's is therefore a good example of a blend of Romanesque and late Gothic styles.

The Käppele (Small Chapel)

Around 1640 a fisherman's son took a carved pietá and placed it on a wayside shrine on the Nikolausberg. Soon the carving was protected by a primitive roof. Shephards and winegrowers, who were at home on the hill, began to stop and pray in front of the shrine. It was not long before the hill became a regular place of pilgrimage and collection plates were brimming over. A pilgrimage chapel was completed in 1684 but the Prince-Bishop at that time insisting that there was nothing miraculous about the spot, refused to acknowledge this chapel until miracles suddenly began to take place. Thereupon, the Prince-Bishop changed his mind. Pilgrims continued to throng up the Nikolausberg especially on religious holidays honoring the Blessed Virgin. In 1747 the Prince-Bishop contracted Balthasar Neumann to build a church west of the chapel. Neumann's plans included a square sanctuary with the choir to the south and chapels off to the west and the east (the original chapel was incorporated into the construction). Two slender towers with gilded crosses above their cupolas decorate the north facade with its clear division of lines. In the niche above the portal the Virgin Mary stands with a lustrous wreath bearing Christ's name across her lap. Adorned by plane trees, the double flight of stairs leading up to the Käppele provides the natural link between the town and the small chapel. Johann Peter Wagner created the Rococo stations of the cross in which Christ's path to Calvary is dramatically reinacted.

La Vieille Ville

Impressions sur une ville

Dom: Cathédrale

Au beau milieu de la vieille ville la cathédrale, le «Dom», forme une grande croix couchée flanquée de quatre tours élancées. Vu de l'extérieur, c'est un bâtiment roman auquel seule la chapelle des Schönborn, elle aussi construite par Balthasar Neumann, ajoute une note baroque. A l'intérieur neuf siècles ont laissé maintes traces: baptistère de bronze daté de 1279, dentelle de fer forgé formant grille à l'entrée (1752), nombreuses pierres tombales des évêques dans la nef, nefs latérales aux riches décorations de stuc contrastant avec la modernité de l'autel, puis au sud le cloître gothique. L'ensemble est éclairé de vitraux modernes faisant la symbiose entre les restes sauvés après l'incendie de la nuit du 16 mars 1945 et une reconstruction qui, au premier abord, ne semblait pas trop problémetique. Quand, en février 1946, la voûte de la nef centrale s'effondra, entraînant maint autre affaissement d'importance, on finit par se décider pour un plafond de bois plat, comme celui de la cathédrale romane. Ce n'est qu'en 1967 que la rénovation de la cathédrale, vouée à St Kilian, Kolonat et Totnan, put être considérée comme achevée.

Neumünster

Non loin du «Dom» une magnifique église baroque, «Neumünster» (1711-1719), dont la coupole majestueuse est reconnaissable de loin, attire surtout les amateurs d'art. C'est de là que chaque année, au mois d'août, depuis le Moyen Age, des pélerins qui vont à pied au Kreuzberg dans la Rhön partent; ils y reviennent quatre jours plus tard, salués au passage par la population. Les reliques de Kilian, Totnan et Kolonat, auxquelles on n'a accès qu'une semaine en juillet, sont conservées dans la crypte.

Marienkapelle: chapelle de la Vierge

Lorsqu'en 1348 la peste noire décima les villes européennes, les Würzbourgeois qui avaient remarqué que les Juifs étaient moins atteints, se hâtèrent de les déclarer responsables et coupables d'avoir empoisonné les puits, et c'est ainsi que le 21 avril 1349 le quartier juif fut tout entier la proie des flammes alors que, dans les maisons avoisinantes, les petites gens se réjouissaient de voir brûler prêteurs, quittances et reconnaissances de dettes. A l'emplacement de la synagogue, l'évêque fit édifier en «purification des lieux» une chapelle de la Vierge, la «Marienkapelle», dont la construction commencée en 1377 traîna en longueur car elle devait être financée par des dons à une époque où les guerres intestines avaient bien appauvri le peuple. Le choeur fut certes terminé dès 1393, mais la nef centrale ne vit son achèvement qu'en 1441. Depuis lors des échoppes, comme on les voit aujourd'hui encore, se nichèrent contre ses flancs. La chapelle ne fut achevée qu'en 1470; plus tard des flèches baroques puis néo-gothiques remplaceront les tours détruites par la foudre. Les amateurs d'art remarquent surtout Adam et Eve qui font face au marché et dont les originaux de Tilman Riemenschneider sont au Mainfränkischen Museum de la forteresse. Les autres statues, de belles pierres tombales dont celle d'un chevalier mort en revenant de croisade est même l'œuvre de Riemenschneider, sans oublier les tympans de la chapelle, tout mérite d'être mentionné et admiré.

Falkenhaus: maison au faucon

Tout à côté, la «Falkenhaus» (la maison au faucon) la plus belle maison patricienne de la ville doit sa façade baroque à un artiste de Haute Bavière qui orna fenêtres et façade de petits amours et de cartouches en stuc à la demande de la veuve d'un riche négociant qui se vit exemptée d'impôts par la ville pour avoir ainsi contribué à l'embellissement de celle-ci. Au premier étage, la Vierge Marie couronnée par les anges, et tout en haut, sur le pignon central, un faucon doré, emblème de la maison qui fut édifiée lors d'une époque de paix et de prospérité qui trouva sa fin brusque et tragique en 1789.

Juliusspital

Quand Julius Echter devint Prince Évêque, Würzburg venait de subir une dure année de famine et d'épidémies. La détresse était grande, c'est pourquoi il fonda en 1576 un hôpital et un hospice de vieillards fort modernes ayant pour but de s'occuper des plus démunis. Jusqu'à la sécularisation cette fondation hébergeait aussi pour trois jours, des pélerins, de pauvres lycéens, des étudiants, voire même des orphelins. Toutes ces bonnes oeuvres étant financées par les bois, vignobles et champs en possession de la fondation qui entretenait également un moulin, une boulangerie et une propre pharmacie. Cette dernière, à l'intérieur du plus pur style rocaille, échappa sous les arcades à l'incendie de 1945. Le bâtiment est un long rectangle de deux cents mètres, l'aile sud borde la Juliuspromenade tandis que l'aile nord fut reconstruite en 1704 d'après les plans d'Antonio Petrini et de Joseph Greising. Julius Echter qui craignait pour ses jeunes boursiers, futurs prêtres, clercs ou médecins, l'influence néfaste de facultés hors de Würzburg créa, en 1582, une université à

Würzburg même. Dans ce bâtiment se trouvaient réunies les quatre facultés de l'époque. C'était des Jésuites qui étaient chargés des cours de théologie et de philosophie. La messe quotidienne était suivie par professeurs et étudiants dans l'église adjacente «Neubaukirche» que Julius Echter fit également contruire. Sa flèche de grès rouge, la plus haute de Würzburg avec ses 79 mètres, s'élève fièrement dans le ciel, même si de nos jours ce sanctuaire désaffecté n'est plus qu'une salle profane de l'université.

Grafeneckart: Hôtel de ville

La tour de l'hôtel de ville, «Grafeneckart», elle, ne mesure que 55 m. Elle abrite la cloche qui servait à annoncer les incendies ou l'approche de l'ennemi. L'arbre peint sur la façade est un souvenir des premières cours de justice tenues sous un tilleul. L'ensemble du complexe témoigne de plusieurs agrandissements au cours des siècles, l'aile qui borde la Karmelitenstrasse fut, par exemple, achevée en stye néorenaissance en 1898. La salle du conseil est ornée d'une gigantesque fresque de Wolfgang Lenz relatant l'histoire de la ville jusqu'à nos jours.

Alte Mainbrücke: vieux pont sur le Main

En 1133 le vieux pont sur le Main, «Alte Mainbrücke» devait sembler aux habitants de Würzburg un miracle de la technique avec ses vastes arches qui résistent tant aux crues qu'à la fonte des neiges charriant des blocs de glace, même si certaines piles durent être réparées après les inondations de 1342 et 1442. C'est le seul pont de cette époque qui soit encore ouvert à la circulation des voitures. Il évoque irrésistiblement son jeune cousin, le Pont Charles de Prague, lui aussi orné de statues baroques. Celles de Würzburg mesurent 4,5 m de haut et représentent, outre L'Immaculée Conception, patronne de la Franconie, et les trois saints irlandais Kilian, Totnan et Kolonat qui évangélisèrent la région, les personnages de Burkart et Bruno vénérés dans le diocèse. Sur l'autre rive, Saint Joseph et L'Enfant Jésus font face à la Vierge, puis Saint Frédéric, Charles Borromée et Népomucène, finalement Charlemagne et Pépin qui envoya à Rome le premier évêque de Würzburg, Burkart, avec l'abbé de St Denis «au sujet des rois de France qui n'avaient pas encore l'autorité royale, pour savoir si c'était bien ou pas». Le Pape Zacharias ayant répondu «qu'il valait mieux que fût nommé roi celui qui avait le pouvoir», cela permit à Pépin de se faire élire roi après avoir fait enfermer dans un monastère, en 751, le dernier roi mérovingien, Childéric III.

Alter Kranen: vieux Crône

Ce pont, ancienne voie empruntée par les Habsbourg pour aller se faire couronner à Francfort réunit depuis 850 ans les deux rives du Main et offre deux beaux panoramas: à l'est le vieux Crône «Alten Kranen» se découpe sur les vignobles. Ce bâtiment, ancien chef-d'oeuvre de la technique, n'est plus en fonction depuis belle lurette mais il est devenu un des emblèmes de la ville avec sa silhouette trapue et ses deux bras de grue capables de charger et décharger simultanément les bateaux et charettes. A l'ouest sur la rive gauche, la forteresse s'élève au-dessus du vieux quartier St Burkard dont l'église conserve, entre d'autres remarquables trésors de l'art plastique, une Madone à l'Enfant Jésus de Riemenschneider. Puis le regard rencontre, dans un écrin de verdure, sur une autre colline à l'est, le «Nikolausberg» la forme blanche, aux tours couronnées de minces bulbes et de croix dorées, de la Käppele.

Käppele

Construite en 1778 par Balthasar Neumann sur l'emplacement d'un très ancien lieu de pélerinage, on y accède aujourd'hui par un vaste escalier double, ombragé de vieux platanes et aménagé en chemin de croix aux stations en terrasses décorées par Johann Peter Wagner qui relient la chapelle et le cloître des Capucins adjacent, à la ville située tout au fond de la cuvette. Les pélerins que les nombreuses statues baroques ne détournaient point de la pieuse récitation de leurs chapelets arrivaient dans la sombre et simple chapelle de grâces pleine d'ex-votos et de représentations en cire des membres guéris par l'intervention de Notre-Dame, témoins naïfs d'une pieuse époque révolue. Elle contraste d'autant plus avec l'intérieur de la Käppele marqué par la richesse baroque, les marbres, les ors, les stucs en rocaille, les angelots et une riche iconographie, sans parler du tabernacle. Quiconque assiste de nos jours encore à la première messe de cinq heures, un dimanche d'été, ou aux offices du mois de Marie, en mai, quand les puissantes orgues accompagnent les cantiques entonnés en l'honneur de la Vierge à la lueur des cierges, comprend l'enracinement profond du culte de la Vierge «en son duché».

Du haut de la terrasse s'offre à nos yeux émerveillés un magnifique panorama sur la ville dont le coeur est entouré d'une «verte ceinture de parcs».

Festung

Bollwerk vergangener Tage

Abendsonne über der Festung. Aus der Dachlandschaft ragen die Türme mit goldenen Kreuzen oder Heiligen. Ein Anblick von majestätischer Größe.

Towers bearing crosses and madonnas soar majestically over the roofs of the fortress in the pale moonlight.

Au-dessus de l'enchevêtrement des toitures de la forteresse et des tours surmontées de croix et de saints, le soleil couchant.

Die Festung Marienberg

Dieser Berg, der erstmals 1172 Marienberg genannt wird, war für die keltische Bevölkerung um 1000 v. Chr. die ideale Zuflucht. Hundert Meter über der Furt am Main gelegen, zu der die Wege zogen, durch Steilhänge nach drei Seiten gesichert, mußte der keltische Ringwall nur nach Westen hin verstärkt werden. Hierher flüchtete man bei Kriegsgefahr mit Vieh und Vorräten aus den Siedlungskernen, die an Quellen lagen.

Um 500 v. Chr. muß wohl ein keltischer Adeliger auf dem Berg gewohnt haben, denn man fand Fragmente eines Weinmischkruges und zweier Trinkschalen, die um 530 v. Chr. in einer Töpferei auf Attika geformt worden waren. Über Marseille und das Rhonetal kamen die kostbaren Gefäße aus Griechenland bis nach Würzburg, dem bisher nördlichsten Fundort dieser Handelsgüter.

Im ersten Jahrhundert nach Chr. drangen Germanenstämme an den mittleren Main vor und unterwarfen die keltischen Bojer. Zuerst kamen die Sweben und die Markomannen, dann die Alemannen, dann die Burgunder und schließlich die Thüringer. Dabei zogen die Stämme nicht restlos ab, wenn sie zum Limes und zum Rhein gedrängt wurden, viele Familien ließen sich überrollen. Zuletzt drangen die Franken von Westen her ins Mainland vor, nachdem sie 496 die Alemannen bei Zülpich und 531 die Thüringer bei Burgscheidungen an der Unstrut besiegt hatten. Die Würzburg wurde Mittelpunkt dieses ostfränkischen Kolonialgebietes und Sitz der Herzöge, die von den Merowingern eingesetzt wurden. Ihre Hofhaltung lag schon rechtsmainisch beim heutigen Domvorplatz, die Befestigung auf dem Berg war Rückhalt und Zuflucht in kriegerischer Zeit.

Die Marienkirche auf dem Marienberg

Daß es in diesem Stützpunkt ein heidnisches Heiligtum gegeben hat, ist wahrscheinlich, wenn auch nicht bezeugt. Herzog Hetan II., Gosberts Sohn, errichtete 706 eine Marienkirche auf dem Berg, wobei er dem Brauch folgte, eine germanische Mutter-Gottheit, vermutlich Hulda, durch die Gottesmutter zu verdrängen. Es wurde die älteste Rundkirche rechts des Rheines, deren 3,50 Meter starke Mauern genügend Schutz boten. In die Krypta wurden 752 die Reliquien der Frankenmärtyrer überführt, die 788 dann in feierlicher Prozession, an der Karl der Große teilnahm, zum Salvatordom geleitet wurden. Mit Hetans II. Tod um 716 erlosch das Herzoghaus. Berg und Kirche fielen an den König zurück, so daß Karlmann, der Hausmeier der Merowinger, sie 741/42 dem von Bonifatius gegründeten Bistum übergeben konnte. Nachdem Bischof Hugo 985 das Burkarduskloster reformiert hatte, schenkte er ihm die „Pfarrkirche auf dem Berge".

Seit 1151, als Bischof Siegfried starb und sein Herz im Kloster Ebrach (seine Gründung) beigesetzt wurde, hat man die Herzen der Würzburger Bischöfe hinter dem Hochaltar der Ebracher Klosterkirche eingemauert, die Eingeweide aber im Boden der Marienkirche auf dem Marienberg bestattet. Erst Julius Echter (†1617) beendete diesen Brauch. Er ließ sein Herz in einem Pfeiler der Universitätskirche einmauern.

Zur Hofkirche wurde die Marienkirche ab 1603 unter Julius Echter umgebaut, der durch Michael Kern das festliche Portal ausführen ließ. Petrus und Paulus flankieren es, vor dem Fenster darüber erscheint die Verkündigung, ganz oben steht Maria zwischen Kilian und Burkard. Weiße Stukkaturen auf blauem Grund schmücken den oberen Teil der Rotunde. Überlebensgroß ist die Verkündigung dargestellt, dazu die Werke der Barmherzigkeit, zwischen den Rippen der Kuppel der Schmerzensmann und Engel mit den Leidenswerkzeugen. Um Platz für seine feierlichen Gottesdienste zu gewinnen, fügte Echter einen größeren Chor an und ließ auf der Evangelienseite eine stuckverzierte Loge einbauen, in die er trokkenen Fußes aus seinen Gemächern gelangen konnte.

Die Ecktürme der Festung flankieren den Fürstenbau oberhalb des Fürstengartens. Der trutzige Bau über der Stadt mit seinen mächtigen Mauern, war immer ein Symbol von Macht und Wohlstand der Fürstbischöfe.

The corner towers of the fortress Marienberg facing the city rise above the princely garden. To the Prince-Bishops, this mighty fortification above the town was the symbol of power and prosperity.

Les tours d'angle de la forteresse flanquent le bâtiment princier du côté de la ville, au-dessus du jardin princier (Fürstengarten), autrefois seul lieu de repos. Le bâtiment massif et ses remparts qui surmontent la ville symbolisaient la puissance et la prospérité des princes-évêques.

Der Bergfried

Bischof Konrad von Querfurt, der 1201 mit dem Ausbau der mittelalterlichen Burg begann, ließ auch den „Wartturm“ anfangen, der wie die Mauern mit Steinen hochgeführt wurde, die man beim Tieferlegen des Halsgrabens abtrug. Da er rund gemauert war, prallten die meisten Wurfgeschosse ab. Aus dreißig Meter Höhe übersahen die Wächter das Umland, während in den Untergeschossen die politischen Häftlinge und Verbrecher einsaßen, die durchs „Angstloch“ auf einem Reitknebel hinabgelassen oder heraufgeholt wurden. Als sich 1408 das Domkapitel gegen eine Steuer wehrte, ließ Bischof Egloffstein aus einer Prozession heraus 13 Domkapitulare verhaften und acht in den großen Turm, fünf in den Randersakkerer Turm werfen.

Die Burg als Bischofssitz

Bischof Hermann von Lobdeburg, der einen neuen Palast bauen ließ, zog sich schon 1242 auf den Marienberg zurück, denn jetzt begannen die Auseinandersetzungen zwischen Bischof und Bürgerschaft. Während sie, wie die meisten Städte des Reichs, auf der Seite des exkommunizierten Kaisers Friedrich II. stand, hielt Bischof Hermann mit den meisten Bischöfen zum Papst. Da die Würzburger Bürger im Mai 1246 die Tore verschlossen hielten, mußten die „Päpstlichen“ auf einer Wiese in Veitshöchheim den Landgrafen Heinrich Raspe zum Gegenkönig wählen. Zum ersten blutigen Zusammenstoß kam es 1253, als die Bürger rechtzeitig erfuhren, daß Bischof Hermann mit einem Gewaltstreich ihren Widerstand brechen wollte. Sie besetzten das Brückentor und schlugen die vom Marienberg in die Stadt reitende Ritterschaft zurück, verhafteten den Bischof im Saalhof neben dem Dom und verlangten, bei der

Den Zugang zum inneren Burghof verwehrte das Scherenbergtor neben dem massigen Kiliansturm, der auf seiner Spitze die vergoldete Statue des Patrons aller Franken trägt.

The Scherenberg Gate along with the Kiliansturm which proudly displays the golden statue of the Franconian patron saint prohibit entry into the inner courtyard of the fortress.

La porte Scherenbergtor, d'aspect rébarbatif, défendait l'entrée de la cour intérieure. A côté d'elle, l'énorme masse de la tour de Kilian qui porte la statue dorée du saint, patron de tous les habitants de la Franconie.

Burg angelangt, deren Übergabe, um sie zu zerstören. Da die Besatzung von einem Gefangenen keine Befahle annehmen wollte, band man den Bischof los. Durch einen Ausfall der Burgleute wurde er in Sicherheit gebracht. Er verließ zu Lebzeiten die Burg nicht mehr.

Seitdem residierten die Bischöfe auf dem Marienberg und übertrugen Burghauptleuten die Verteidigung, die stets 30 Reiter und zehn Bogenschützen zur Verfügung hatten. Als die Bürger am Ende der Tellsteige eine Mauer mit einem Tor errichtet hatten, um den Zugang zur Burg zu kontrollieren, ließ Bischof Andreas von Gundelfingen am Fasnachtsabend 1308 die Belagerer verjagen und erschlagen. Er brachte die Stadt in die Reichsacht, weil ihm die Rädelsführer nicht ausgeliefert wurden.

Das Brunnenhaus

Als die Bauernhaufen im Mai 1525 den Marienberg belagerten, rissen sie die Bleiröhren der Wasserleitung heraus, die Quellwasser von Höchberg in die Burg lieferte. Die belagerten „Bischöflichen" unter Sebastian von Rotenhan hätten bald kapitulieren müssen, hätten sie nicht über den tiefen Brunnen verfügt. In mühseliger Arbeit war ein 103 Meter tiefer Schacht in den Muschelkalk niedergebracht worden. Die Sohle wird nicht durch Sickerwasser oder gar von Mainwasser gespeist, sondern von zwei dort austretenden Quellen. Mit einer Pumpe oder einem Tretrad holte man das saubere Wasser herauf.

Den achtseitigen Brunnentempel ließ erst Julius Echter vor 1603 durch den Nürnberger Jakob Wolff bauen. Von einer häßlichen Ummantelung 1937 befreit, ist das Brunnenhaus ein hervorragendes Zeugnis der mainfränkischen Renaissance. Über dem Wasserbecken an der Ostseite steht Herkules (oder Simson), der dem Löwen den Rachen aufreißt, in den Nischen seitlich davon sind die Propheten Daniel und Hieronymus dargestellt. Auf dem Dach jedoch schwebt auf goldener Kugel Fortuna, die Glücksgöttin, 1938 von Fried Heuler nach einem Stich in der Festschrift von 1603 gestaltet.

Scherenbergtor und Hofstube

Fürstbischof Rudolf von Scherenberg, der 1466 im 65. Lebensjahr zum Fürstbischof gewählt worden war, rettete das heillos verschuldete Hochstift durch eiserne Sparsamkeit und neue vom Kaiser gewährte Steuerprivilegien vor dem Konkurs. Das westliche Burgtor, das dann seinen Namen trug, ließ er verstärken und mit Figuren Mariens und der drei Frankenapostel schmücken. In den umgebauten Südflügel veranlaßte er die „Neue Hofstube" einzubauen, einen riesigen Gesindesaal von 30 Meter Länge und 12 Meter Breite, der kürzlich als Tagungssaal wieder erstanden ist.

Die Bauern greifen an

Schon Rudolf von Scherenberg hatte einen Vorgeschmack der Unruhen erhalten, als 1476 an die tausend Wallfahrer von Niklashausen vor die Burg zogen, um den „heiligen Jüngling" Hans Böhm zu befreien. Noch konnte man sie mit einigen Schüssen verscheuchen, die wenigen Bewaffneten im Kirchhof von Waldbüttelbrunn umzingeln und niederkämpfen.

Die Bauern und die Bürger der kleinen Städte im Taubergrund, auf dem Bauland und im Odenwald, im Grabfeld und den Haßbergen kamen 1525 nicht singend und im Schein der Kerzen nach Würzburg. Sie hatten Morgensterne und Spieße, gerade geschmiedete Sensen und etliche Geschütze, die Graf Georg von Wertheim ihnen überlassen hatte. Zu wenige freilich für die starken Mauern, weshalb kriegserfahrene Führer wie Götz von Berlichingen und Florian Geyer von einem Sturm abrieten. Während Florian Geyer nach Rothenburg ritt, um die Bürger zur Herausgabe ihrer Geschütze zu bewegen, begannen die

Der Weg zum Scherenbergtor führt entlang der Südmauer über den 18 Meter tiefen Halsgraben. Unter Bischof Rudolf von Scherenberg wurde die Mauer durch Türme verstärkt, die den typisch fränkischen Ziegelhelm tragen.

The path to the Scherenbergertor (Gate) with the Kilian Tower in the background leads along the southern wall that emerges from an 18-meter deep ditch. During the reign of Bishop Rudolf von Scherenberg, the wall was fortified with towers covered by the style of tile roof that is typically Franconian.

Le chemin menant à la porte Scherenberg et à la tour de Kilian qui s'érige derrière, longe le mur sud construit au-dessus des douves profondes de dix-huit mètres. Sous l'évêque Rudolf von Scherenberg les murailles furent renforcées de tours coiffées du «Ziegelhelm» typiquement franconien.

Zur Not hätte man sich auch in der Marienkirche der Festung verteidigen können. Die starken Mauern der Rundkirche würden genügend Schutz bieten. – Zwischen den beiden Kaskadenbrunnen des Fürstengartens wurden acht Blumenparterres und ein Springbrunnen angelegt, eine Augenweide der höfischen Gesellschaft. Von hier aus trägt der Blick weit über die Stadt.

In an emergency refuge could also be sought in the Marienkirche (church) in the Marienberg fortress. – Eight flower beds and a fountain were laid out between the cascade fountains of the Fürstengarten – a pleasure garden for the court society.

En cas de danger on aurait pu se défendre dans l'église Marienkirche de la forteresse. Huit parterres de fleurs et le jet d'eau d'une fontaine, entre les deux fontaines à cascades, réjouissaient les regards de la Cour. De là aussi s'étend un magnifique panorama sur la ville et ses environs.

Bauernhaufen am Abend des 15. Mai 1525 unter Trommel- und Pfeifenklang und bei fliegenden Fahnen den Sturm auf die Schotenflanke, die Nordseite der Burg. Sie konnten die äußeren Pallisaden überwinden und legten im Graben schon Leitern an, da flogen Steine, Pechkränze und Feuerkugeln auf sie herab, bis sie elend im Graben umkamen. Auch ein zweiter Sturm in der Dunkelheit scheiterte ebenso wie Tage später der Versuch, bei St. Burkard einen Stollen in den Fels zu treiben und den Marienberg in die Luft zu jagen.

Julius Echter wandelt die Burg in ein Schloß um

Beim Ausbau zum repräsentativen Schloß durfte die Wehrhaftigkeit nicht vernachlässigt werden, denn bei den starken Spannungen zwischen den katholischen und den protestantisch reformierten Staaten konnte es Jahr für Jahr zum Konflikt kommen. Die Pläne für die Um- und Neubauten stammen von Jakob Wolff, der von Nürnberg wochenweise „ausgeliehen" wurde. Er ließ im Nordosteck den Marienturm aufmauern, dann den Nordflügel neu errichten und schließlich am Nordwesteck den Kiliansturm bauen.

Die Innenausstattung, vor allem der Kaiserzimmer im Nordosten des Schlosses übernahm Endres Jäger aus Ulm, doch wurden sie bis auf geringe Reste zerstört. Alles, was nicht niet- und nagelfest war, wurde 1631 als Beutegut weggeschleppt, die Gold- und Silberarbeiten des Kunstkabinetts in handliche Stücke zerschlagen, die etwa 3000 in Leder gebundenen Bücher der Bibliothek auf Weisung König Gustav Adolfs nach Uppsala, der einzigen Universität Schwedens, verbracht.

Die vergrößerte Hofhaltung erforderte jenseits des tiefen Halsgrabens einen zweiten Hof, den im Süden und Norden Wirt-

So geschlossen und wehrhaft sahen die Gegner, die aus Westen kamen, die Festung. – Und so (auf dem Bild rechts oben) erblickten die Städter die steinerne Krone des Herzogtums.

Enemies approaching from the west saw the fortress as a structure of solid fortification. – The town dwellers felt the same about the stone crown of the Duchy.

Les adversaires qui venaient de l'ouest voyaient la forteresse aussi fermée qu'imprenable; et c'est ainsi que les habitants de la ville voyaient la couronne de pierres du duché (photo en haut à droite).

schaftsgebäude begrenzen, dem im Westen aber zwei Basteien als Bollwerk vorgebaut wurden, um die Angriffsseite zu decken. Aus dem roten Mainsandstein, aus dem die große Pferdeschwemme im Hof errichtet wurde, meißelte Michael Kern die Figur des hl. Michael, das Symbol der Gegenreformation, die, über dem Tor aufgestellt, dem nächsten Feind entgegenblickte.

Aus dem Schloß wird eine Festung

Gestiefelt und gespornt kam 1642 der kaiserliche Reiteroffizier Johann Philipp von Schönborn zur Bischofswahl, da er sich keine Chance ausrechnete. Er wurde seiner militärischen Kenntnisse wegen gewählt, konnte aber erst nach 1652 beginnen, die Stadt und den Marienberg mit den mächtigen Bastionen zu umgeben, die eine künftige Eroberung unmöglich machen sollten. Schon 1648 sicherte das Neutor den Zugang von Nordosten, 1649 das Schönborntor den Zutritt in den inneren Bereich. Mit 700 Arbeitern wurden unter Schönborn und seinem dritten Nachfolger Johann Gottfried von Guttenberg Bastion um Bastion gebaut.

Das Mainfränkische Museum

Es war ein verwegener Entschluß, 1946 im Zeughaus und Kommandantenbau die geretteten Schätze des ausgebombten Luitpoldmuseums der Stadt Würzburg aufzustellen, denn Benzin war scharf kontingentiert, nur wenige Fahrzeuge zugelassen. Inzwischen hat sich das Museum, vor allem durch seine Sonderausstellungen, einen solchen Ruf erworben, daß jährlich an die 300 000 Besucher auf den Marienberg kommen, um den geretteten Reichtum Würzburgs und Frankens zu betrachten, der inzwischen durch Schenkungen, Käufe und Dauerleihgaben erweitert wurde. Herzstück ist nach wie vor der Saal mit den Figuren Riemenschneiders, des großen Bildschnitzers und Bürgers der Stadt.

Aus den Reichtümern des Mainfränkischen Museums werden hier Werke Tilman Riemenschneiders und der Veit-Stoß-Schule vorgestellt, dazu die Kelterhalle mit Zeugnissen deutscher Weinkultur und Grabmäler im Rittersaal.

Among the many treasures the Mainfränkisches Museum has on display works by Tilman Riemenschneider and the school of Veit Stoß. In addition, there is a wine-pressing room displaying German wine artifacts and knightly effigies.

Parmi toutes les richesses du musée de la forteresse on voit ici deux oeuvres de Tilmann Riemenschneider, puis la «Kelterhalle» avec les nombreux témoignages de la tradition oenologique allemande ainsi que des pierres tombales dans la salle des chevaliers (Rittersaal).

The Fortress

A Monument of Bygone Days

The Fortress Marienberg

This hill which was first officially called Marienberg in 1172, offered the ideal refuge for the Celts who settled here as early as 500 B.C. Germanic tribes settled here too; the Franks liked it so well they made Würzburg their ducal seat and held court near the present day site of the Cathedral. The Marienberg's position – one hundred meters above the Main ford, steep slopes on three sides and thus natural fortification – provided entire settlements protection in times of danger. As of the 13th century, even the bishops of Würzburg retreated to the fortifications atop the hill. Their enemies, however, were not always outside forces; at times, the town's citizens posed a threat as well.

Marienkirche (Mary's Church)

It is most probable that heathens also had a place of worship on the Marienberg before the 3.5 meter thick walls of the church were erected in 706 to honor Mary, Mother of God. This church bore such significance that in 752 the relics of the Franconian martyrs were laid to rest in the crypt of the oldest round church west of the Rhine. In 788 Charlemagne participated in a ceremonious procession in which the relics were carried to the crypt of the Neumünster Church – at the time the site of the Cathedral. As of 1152 the hearts of Würzburg's bishops were emtombed behind the high altar of the monastery church in Ebrach; the entrails, however, were buried in the floor of Mary's Church. Julius Echter first broke with this tradition in 1617 when his heart was preserved in one of the columns of the University Church which he had founded.

Under Julius Echter, the Marienkirche was enlarged and transformed into the Court Church and a decorative Renaissance portal was added. Peter and Paul to the left and the right of the door; in front of the window above, the annunciation.

Bergfried (Castle Keep)

The 30 meter high castle keep (today 42 meters) was begun in 1201 and provided excellent surveillance of the countryside around while the stones from enemy catapults richocheted off its thick rounded stone walls. Political prisoners and criminals were kept locked up in the lower floors.

Brunnenhaus (Fountain House)

If it had not been for the 103 meter deep well that supplied the fortress with fresh spring water, the besieged bishops would have soon had to surrender in Mai 1525 as the peasants laid siege to the Marienberg. In 1603, Julius Echter had the octagonal fountain house built in the beautiful Renaissance style typical of the Main-Franconian region. The elegant building is accentuated by corner columns and decorated with reliefs: Hercules tearing open the mouth of a lion, Daniel in the Lion's Den, and the Prophet Hieronymus with a lion. A Renaissance balustrade crowns the flat roof and the goddess Fortuna stands majestically on a golden ball.

Scherenberg Gate and Quarters

Rudolf von Scherenberg, who in 1466 was elected Prince-Bishop at the age of 65, salvaged the hopelessly indebted bishopric by stringent frugality and the right to tax granted him by the emperor. He had the west gate that now bears his name fortified and adorned it with Franconia's three apostles and the Virgin Mary. He also had the south wing renovated into domestic quarters; today the wing serves as a convention hall.

Julius Echter makes a castle out of the fortress

When Julius Echter became Prince-Bishop in 1573, he began to transform the Marienberg into a stately castle. In doing so, he knew he could not neglect the castle's fortification as tension between the Catholics and the Protestants was mounting. Jakob Wolff was „borrowed" from Nuremberg for weeks at a time to undertake the alterations: the Marienturm and the Kiliansturm (towers) were built up and the northern wing refurbished. Gold and silver embellished the royal apartments. The enlargement of the household meant the addition of a second courtyard and domestic buildings which were protected by two bastions built as bulwarks. The symbol of the Counter-Reformation, the archangel Michael, was carved out of the red sandstone used to build the large horse pond and placed in the center of the Echter Gate. There he could cast a stern eye upon the enemy.

The Swedes take the Marienberg

The bishopric of Würzburg which diligently supported the Catholic military league had been protected against any of the consequences of the Thirty Years' War until King Gustav Adolf of Sweden conquered Count Tilly in 1631 thus opening the doors to Franconia and an attack on the fortress. Having successfully stormed and taken the Marienberg, the king helped himself to the manifold treasures of the castle including a library of over 3000 leatherbound volumes which he had sent to the university in Uppsala. Gustav Adolf then gave his soldiers free reign and they plundered literally every nook and cranny of the fortress leaving virtually nothing behind. Being familiar with the vulnerable points, the Swedes expanded the fortifications but in 1635, Imperial troops recaptured the town and the Swedish troops surrendered after having exhausted all their provisions within the Marienberg.

The castle is reconverted to a fortress

Johann Philipp von Schönborn was elected Prince-Bishop due to his military prowess and in 1652 he began to surround the town and the Marienberg with formidable bastions in order to ensure that the fortress could never be captured again. Seven hundred men were put to work constructing bastion upon bastion (3 deep) on the west side. However well-armed for attack, the Prince-Bishops remained untouched by war and yet martial construction continued – in 1708 a huge arsenal and headquarters building were begun whereby the artillery park and the cellar directly below it were both over 100 meters in length and had freestanding vaulted ceilings. The arsenal was said to be equipped with everything Mars and Bellona could have desired while the cellar contained all that an army of drinkers could wish for – 160 cannons and keg upon keg of wine. The year 1724 saw the beginning of construction on the Maschikulturm (Maschicolation Tower) halfway up the southwest slope known as the Leistengrund. Cannons could be fired out of 9 loopholes in the artillery gallery, 8 loopholes were on the first level and again 9 on the second. The breastwork contained 22 embrasures and hoardings that enabled shots to be fired directly to the base of the tower. The tower was never put to the test even though French troops did occupy the fortress in 1800 and again in 1813/14. When Prussian artillery sent the arsenal and headquarters building up in flames in 1866, it was finally realized that the fortress Marienberg had outlived its time. It was turned into a barracks.

Mainfränkisches Museum

It was a bold undertaking in 1946 to move the rescued museum treasures out of the bombed city to the arsenal and headquarters building on the Marienberg. In the meantime, through the assistance of private donations, purchases and extended loans, the rich treasures of Würzburg and Franconia have made a name for the museum.

La forteresse

Fortifications d'antan

Cette colline appelée pour la première fois «colline de Marie» (Marienberg) en 1172 était déjà mille ans av. J-C un refuge idéal pour les populations celtes de pêcheurs et cultivateurs établies à cet endroit où le Main est guéable. Des fragments de poteries grecques y attestent même la présence de riches Celtes 500 ans av. J.C. Après quoi on vit déferler, les unes après les autres, des tribus de Germains avant que Würzburg ne devienne le centre de la Franconie orientale, siège des ducs investis par les Mérovingiens résidant sur la rive droite. La «Marienkirche», église de la Vierge, aux murs de 3,50 m d'épaisseur (et la première église ronde sur la rive droite du Rhin), fut construite en 706; elle abrita dans sa crypte les reliques des martyrs avant que celles-ci ne fussent transférées, en présence de Charlemagne, sur la rive droite. Son aspect actuel est dû aux importantes modifications apportées par Julius Echter en 1603.

Le donjon date de 1201, année où l'évêque Konrad von Querfurt commença la construction du château-fort médiéval. Du haut de ses trente mètres, les gardes pouvaient surveiller les alentours, alors que les prisonniers politiques et les malfaiteurs étaient descendus ou remontés par le «trou de la peur» (Angstloch) qui menait dans ses profondeurs. Dès 1242, le château devint siège de l'évêque. Hermann von Lobdeburg, partisan du Pape, s'y réfugia lorsque commença le conflit l'opposant à la ville de Würzburg qui, comme presque toutes les villes de l'Empire, était fidèle à l'Empereur. Après de sanglants combats (1253) l'évêque ne quitta plus la forteresse dont la défense était assurée en permanence par trente cavaliers et dix archers, et où résidèrent ses successeurs. Dans la Tour de Randersacker furent emprisonnés en 1525 soixante bourgeois de la ville, parmi eux Tilman Riemenschneider, qui avaient pris part à la guerre des paysans. La porte «Scherenbergtor» ainsi que l'aile sud datent du XVième siècle.

La forteresse fut attaquée, sans succès, par les paysans dans la nuit du 15 mai 1525 au cours des meurtrières luttes seigneuriales de cette époque et ce n'est que sous Julius Echter, de 1573 à 1617, qu'il y eut une trêve permettant des aménagements au château, sans pour autant négliger les fortifications d'ailleurs. On adjoignit alors aux constructions une seconde cour, des bastions et le grand abreuvoir à chevaux surmonté de St Michel terrassant le dragon, symbole de la contre-réforme. En 1631 les troupes suédoises qui pillèrent la ville réussirent aussi à s'emparer de la forteresse qui se vit encore agrandie après l'élection, en 1642, de Johann Philipp von Schönborn au poste de prince-évêque; depuis lors les caves recèlent des milliers de litres de vin à côté de cent soixante canons. Ni en 1796, quand les troupes révolutionnaires françaises commandées par Jourdan occupent la ville, ni en 1812-1813, la forteresse ne fut attaquée et sa fonction se révéla définitivement dépassée en 1866, quand l'artillerie prussienne mit le feu à certains bâtiments. Elle ne servit plus alors que de caserne.

Transporter à la forteresse en 1946, alors qu'essence et véhicules étaient denrées rares, les trésors du musée Luitpold qui avaient pu être sauvés, témoigne d'une certaine audace. Entre-temps le musée de la forteresse a acquis une grande popularité avec trois cent mille visiteurs chaque année; ils viennent admirer les expositions temporaires ou les collections dont les statues de Riemenschneider restent le joyau incontesté.

Vom Wein

Tradition und Lebensfreude

Über den Rebzeilen der Weinbergslage „Innere Leiste" droht der Kanonenturm, der nach den Pechnasen Maschikuliturm heißt. Von Maximilian von Welsch geplant, wurde er von Balthasar Neumann ab 1724 erbaut.

The gun tower that poses a threat to the vineyards „Innere Leiste" is named Machicolation Tower because of the decorative projecting works at the top of the tower. The tower was planned by Maximilian von Welsch and Balthasar Neumann started its construction in 1724.

Au dessus des ceps du vignoble «Innere Leiste», la tour canonnière, appelée tour des machicoulis. Sa construction, décidée par Maximilian von Welsch, fut réalisée par Balthasar Neumann à partir de 1724.

Vom Weinbau in Würzburg ist erstmals 779 in einer Urkunde die Rede. Damals gingen ortsansässige freie Franken um die Würzburger Gemarkung rechts des Maines und kamen dabei durch den Weingarten des „Fredthant" (ein freier Weinbauer).

Klöster und Stifte (geistliche Stiftungen) waren Leuten wie Fredthant im Weinbau bald überlegen, denn ihnen war nach der benediktinischen Regel aufgetragen, ihr Kloster oder Stift wirtschaftlich unabhängig zu machen. Erst als durch Schenkungen oft weit entfernte Weingärten ans Kloster kamen, mußte man Laien einsetzen, oft an den Boden gebundene Halb- und Unfreie. Entscheidend für den Erfolg der geistlichen Weingüter war jedoch der Informationsvorsprung, denn sie kannten in Abschriften die wenigen aus der Antike überlieferten Werke über Garten- und Weinbau, die in Latein, der alleinigen Urkunden- und Buchsprache abgefaßt waren.

Ihr Besitz an Weinbergen mehrte sich, denn bis weit in die Neuzeit hinein wurden Weinberge oder wenigstens die Jahreszinsen daraus gestiftet. Als Gegengabe wurde meist die Ausrichtung der Jahrtage verlangt oder ein Licht in der Kirche. „Um meines Seelenheiles willen", so begründet der Bürger Alpin 1094 seine Schenkung zum Altar des hl. Petrus im Kloster St. Stephan. Wurden zunächst die „alten" Klöster beschenkt wie St. Burkard und St. Stephan, dazu die Stifte Haug und Neumünster, so brachten es später in Würzburg einziehende Orden auch noch zu stattlichem Besitz. Daneben fanden die einheimischen Häcker beengten Platz, mußten nach Mißernten ihre Grundstücke verschulden.

Von alters her galt der „Stein", ein riesiger Südhang, als die beste Lage. Eimerweise (1 Eimer = 78,4 l) ließ sich Goethe Steinwein nach Weimar schicken und war „verdrüßlich", wenn er seine Bouteille Steinwein nicht genießen konnte. E. T. A. Hoffmann, der Leistenwein bevorzugte, klagte gelegentlich

Der pflanzengrüne, im Sommer kühle Hof des „Stachel" gehört zur ältesten erhaltenen Weinwirtschaft (1413) Würzburgs, in der 1525 die Bauernhauptleute tagten und den Sturm auf die Festung beschlossen.

One of the loveliest features of „Stachel", one of the oldest remaining inns dating back to 1413, is the romantic courtyard adorned with climbing ivy and oleander bushes that make it a cool and inviting place on a warm summer evening. „Stachel" is where the peasants gathered in 1525 to plan their attack on the fortress Marienberg.

La fraîche cour intérieure verdoyante du «Stachel» est celle de la plus vieille taverne de la ville, datant de 1413, dans laquelle se réunirent, en 1525, les chefs des paysans pour décider de monter à l'attaque de la forteresse Marienberg.

Die Gewölbe unter der Residenz waren von alters her dem Ausbau der Weine vorbehalten, die dem Fürstbischof, dann den Königen von Bayern, schließlich dem Freistaat Bayern zustanden. Weinproben bei Kerzenschimmer zwischen den alten Holzfässern gehören mit zu den schönsten Erinnerungen an Würzburg.

The vaulted cellars under the Residenz have always served as a winery; first for the Prince-Bishops, then for the Bavarian kings and today, for the free state of Bavaria. With the wooden vats as a fitting backdrop, wine-tasting by candlelight is a speciality of the large wineries in Würzburg.

Depuis toujours les caves voûtées sous la Résidence étaient réservées aux tonneaux des vins provenant des propriétés du prince-évêque, puis du roi de Bavière et finalement de l'Etat libre de Bavière. Les vins des plus grands vignobles de Würzburg font l'objet de dégustations à la lueur des chandelles entre les vieux foudres.

über einen benommenen Kopf am Tag darauf, was nicht verwunderlich war, denn zu seiner Zeit kannte man noch keine Sortenreinheit im Weinberg. Der Mischbestand überstand leichter die Fröste und lieferte auch in schlechten Jahren etwas Ertrag.

Erst in der Biedermeierzeit entwickelte man den Qualitätsweinbau. Sortenrein zog man jetzt Silvaner, den Abt Alberich Degen von Ebrach erstmals am „Stein" hatte pflanzen lassen, oder rheinischen Riesling, den Sekretär Nickels 1826 aus Geisenheim kommen ließ. Man gab das tiefe Wenden auf, ließ nur noch eine Pflanze pro Stock zu und bestimmte das Mostgewicht mit der Öchslewaage, was der Kundschaft mitgeteilt wurde. Führend bei Qualitätsanbau und Absatz waren die drei großen Weingüter in Würzburg. Das älteste ist das des Bürgerspitals, dem der Stifter Johann von Steren 1321, nur zwei Jahre nach der Gründung, bereits 13 Morgen Weinberg „im Sand" und „im Lindach" schenkte „den Kranken und Schwachen zur Lab und Stärkung". Noch heute wird den 45 im Spital wohnenden Pfründern täglich ein Schoppen Wein, sonntags aber zwei gereicht. Durch Zustiftungen und Käufe wurde das Rebland auf 140 Hektar erweitert, wovon der größte Teil auf Würzburger Gemarkung liegt. Um Weinfälscher auszuschalten, die ihre Mixturen auch in Bocksbeutel abfüllten, wurden die Bocksbeutel des Bürgerspitals seit 1726 konsequent mit dem Ratssiegel „verpetschiert".

Den Grundstock zum Juliusspital-Weingut legte Julius Echter 1577, als er vier Morgen am Marsberg in Randersacker, vier Morgen an der Heinrichsleite den „Armen in meinem Spital zu deren Erquickung" schenkte. Auch hier gab es Zustifter und gute Käufe. Inzwischen verfügt die Stiftung über 60 Hektar Rebland in der Würzburger Gemarkung und weitere 107 Hektar im Fränkischen. Beiden Spitälern reichen die Einnahmen aus dem Weinverkauf nicht mehr, um Altenheime oder die Klinik des Juliusspitals zu unterhalten.

Im Staatsweingut (bis 1919 Hofkellerei genannt) wurde nach der Säkularisation 1803 der Weinbergsbesitz des Fürstbischofs, des Domkapitels, der Klöster und Stifte zusammengefaßt. Als dieser Besitz 1814 endgültig zu Bayern kam, wurden die ältesten Bestände nach München geschafft, so der Jahrgang 1540, der 1631 erfolgreich vor den Schweden versteckt, oder der 1796er, der vor den Franzosen nach Marktsteft geschafft worden war. Außer stattlichem Besitz im Mainfränkischen gehören dem Staatsweingut die Lagen Leisten und Schloßberg allein und tüchtige Anteile an der Abtsleite und am „Stein".

In den Weinstuben der „großen Drei", aber auch in den „gutbürgerlichen" in der Stadt kann jeder in gemütlicher Runde oder als stiller Genießer seine Sorte, seine Lage und seinen Jahrgang herausfinden. Wie er es gelernt hat, prüft er Farbe, Geruch und Geschmack, trinkt schlückchenweise und verschafft sich mit etwas Brot und Käse einen „neuen Gaumen", wenn er zu einem anderen Wein wechselt. Wer nur seinen Durst löschen will, hält sich an das landesübliche „Schorle", eine Mischung aus einem Achtel Wein und einem Achtel Mineralwasser, die Marschall Augereau den Würzburgern um 1811 mit dem Spruch „Toujour l'amour" empfohlen haben soll. Daraus wurde durch Endsilbenverschlucken das „Schorle".

Dicht gedrängt beim Hoffest des Bürgerspitals oder in familiärer Atmosphäre in einem Weinlokal. Es heißt, daß Essen und Trinken Leib und Seele zusammenhalten.

Whether in the crowded courtyard of the Bürgerspital's Hoffest (wine festival) or in the cosier atmosphere of an inn, the proverb goes that food and drink keep body and soul together.

Côte à côte, et même coude à coude, lors de la fête du vin dans la cour du Bürgerspital ou dans l'atmosphère familière d'une taverne. Il faut que le boire et le manger réjouissent le corps et l'âme.

Of Wine,
Tradition and the Joys of Life

Winegrowing in Würzburg was first officially mentioned in 779. At that time local freemen planted the hills with their vineyards from Würzburg all along the Main River to Veitshöchheim. Cloisters and religious charitable foundations which were bent on being financially independent began growing wine too and soon had the upper hand. Their capacity for winegrowing continued to increase as these institutions were often endowed with vineyards, some of which were so far away that serfs or bondsmen living in those regions had to be employed. The real advantage, however was their knowledge and know-how, something that had been passed down to them and documented in the few Latin texts on agriculture and viticulture in existence. Annual tithes were usually based on vineyards. In return either a commemoration day was set up or a candle lit in the church: "for the good of my soul" one donor explained in 1094. In the beginning it was mainly the "old" cloisters like St. Burkard that received such tithes but as time passed new orders appeared in Würzburg and they too, could boast of stately vineyards. Thus local winegrowers slowly but surely were not only forced out of competition but often went into debt as well. The broad south slope, the "Stein", today behind the train station, has always been considered the most ideal location for wine growing. Goethe is known to have had "Stein" wine sent to Weimar "by the bucket" (one bucket = 78.4 liters) and he was most upset and vexed when he could not enjoy his bouteille of "Stein". E.T.A. Hoffman, a German Romanticist, sometimes complained of having a hangover the following day which should not have been a surprise as there was no such thing as wine made from one variety of grape. Several different varieties planted together were much more resilient to frost and this was also the reason why even in bad years there was wine to be had. It was not until the nineteenth century that wines could be spoken of as to their quality. Silvaner was the first variety planted on the Stein slope followed by a Riesling from the Rhine valley. Viticulture became somewhat more sophisticated as grape vines were being planted individually according to their variety and as the must density was measured for the first time. The leading vintners in quality wines were the three large winegrowers in Würzburg; the oldest being the Bürgerspital whose endower only two years after its foundation donated 13 acres of vineyards to the weak and the sick to strengthen their earthly bodies. Even today, a fourth of a liter of wine (Sundays a half liter) is part and parcel of the fare for the 45 inhabitants of the old age home. Over the years the Bürgerspital has been endowed with vineyards or has managed to purchase some land on its own so that nowadays it grows wine on 140 hectares, most of which is in and around Würzburg. In order to prevent adulteration, Bürgerspital wines have been subject to testing for quality since 1726 and each Bocksbeutel bottle bears this official seal of approval.

In the 16th century Julius Echter, the founder of the university in Würzburg, donated several acres of vineyards "for the refreshment of the poor in my hospital" (Juliusspital). As was the case with the Bürgerspital, further endowments and purchases led to a total of 60 hectares of vineyards in the Würzburg area and another 107 hectares in Franconia. Today, wine sales are no longer sufficient to keep either of these institutions in a position to totally finance its old age home or hospital. Upon secularization in 1803 the vineyards of the former Prince-Bishops, the Cathedral, the cloisters and other charitable foundations were combined to become a state-owned winery known as the Hofkellerei or Court Cellars since 1919. In 1814 as these cellars were finally firmly in the possession of the Bavarian crown, the rarest of the wines were sent to the capital Munich: a wine from the vintage year 1540 that had successfully been hidden from the Swedes when they attacked Würzburg in 1631 and the '96 (1796) that was gloriously prevented from falling into French hands. This state-run winery has its wine growing on excellent vineyards slopes below the fortress and on the famous "Stein" as well as in several other outlying areas in Franconia. Today, these spacious wine cellars are located in the north and south wings of the Residence.

There is no more appropriate way to feel at home in Würzburg than by spending a few pleasant hours over a "Schoppen" (1/4 liter) of Franconian wine in one of the numerous local wine inns. The above-mentioned trio specializes in serving solely their own wines while other wine pubs offer a wider variety. Drinking a glass of "Frankenwein" is an art in itself: The glass is held by its stem in order to keep the wine free of any impurities. First the color is carefully inspected, then the nose of the variety. Tasting begins with small sips that are washed around in the mouth so that the true flavor has a chance to unfold. Peasant brown bread serves to neutralize the taste buds between varieties. Since Franconian wines are much too noble to be drunk purely as thirst-quenchers, a mixture of half mineral water and half wine (called a "Schorle") is served. The "Schorle" is said to have come from the French Marshall Augereau who upon his visit to Würzburg in 1811 continued to recommend his watered-down wine with the words "toujour L'amour". To the Franconian ear this sounded like "Schorle".

Au sujet du vin

Tradition et joie de vivre

Il est question de vin à Würzburg pour la première fois en 779 et on connaît même le nom d'un propriétaire de l'époque: Fredthant. Mais bientôt ce sont les monastères et les couvents qui, selon la règle bénédictine leur enjoignant de «prier et travailler» pour être indépendants, gagnent en importance. Ce qui est capital pour le succès des hommes d'Eglise, c'est qu'ils avaient accès aux rares textes latins se rapportant à l'art de cultiver jardins et vignobles. Les donations aux monastères les plus anciens n'empêcheront pas des ordres installés bien plus tard d'obtenir, eux aussi, de vastes propriétés alors que les vignerons devaient se contenter de petites parcelles et étaient obligés de s'endetter en cas de mauvaises récoltes.

Depuis toujours le «Stein», un cru poussant sur un versant sud, était le plus coté, et Goethe s'en faisait envoyer à Weimar des «seaux entiers», un seau correspondant à 78,4 litres. E.T.A Hoffmann préférait le vin poussant sur la colline de la forteresse, le «Leisten». Ce n'est qu'au milieu du XIXième siècle que la qualité est sensiblement améliorée et les sortes riesling et sylvaner sont alors introduites.

Les trois grands domaines qui, de tout temps, étaient à la pointe du progrès pour la bonification et la vente des vins sont, de nos jours encore, bien représentés à Würzburg.

Le plus vieux est le «Bürgerspital» dont les vins «fortifient et réjouissent les faibles et les malades». Aujourd'hui encore 45 prébendiers würzbourgeois habitant l'hospice ont droit à un quart de litre par jour et à un demi litre de vin le dimanche. Des achats et donations agrandissent les propriétés (140 ha à Würzburg). Dès 1726 pour éviter les contrefaçons on cachette les bouteilles «Bocksbeutel» aux flancs arrondis typiques des seuls vins de Franconie alors.

C'est Julius Echter qui, en 1577, acheta quelques arpents et fonda le «Juliusspital» pour «offrir aux pauvres de mon hospice leur rafraîchissement». Là aussi des donations et achats judicieux font que la fondation a de nos jours 60 ha à Würzburg et 107 autres en Franconie. Cependant les revenus provenant de la vente du vin ne suffisent plus pour subvenir aux besoins de la maison de retraite ou de l'hôpital.

Après la sécularisation en 1803, les vignobles du clergé passèrent à l'Etat, sous le nom de «Hofkellerei» jusqu'en 1919. Aujourd'hui le «Staatsweingut» dispose d'énormes caves sous la Résidence où il entrepose tant les crus renommés würzbourgeois du «Stein» ou de «Abtsleite», que des vins fameux provenant de toute la région: Randersacker, Handthal, Abtswind, Hammelburg ou Kreuzwertheim, pour n'en citer que quelques uns parmi les plus célèbres; alors qu'en 1814 on avait transporté à Munich les grands millésimes de 1540 et les autres qui avaient pu échaper aux rapines (suédoises de 1631 et françaises de 1796).

Dans les «Weinstube» des trois grands domaines comme dans les nombreuses tavernes de la ville, le vin se déguste à petites gorgées après qu'on en aura examiné la couleur, le bouquet, puis le goût; un peu de pain ou de fromage permettent de «se refaire le palais» avant de passer à une autre sorte. Ceux qui ont soif préfércront un mélange de vin et d'eau minérale en quantités égales: le «Schorle», qui aurait été conseillé en 1811 aux habitants par le Maréchal Augereau disant «toujours l'amour», ce qui, à force d'être raccourci, finit par donner «Shorle».

Veitshöchheim

Lustschloß aus alten Zeiten

Uralte Blutbuchen stehen wie Wächter um das fürstbischöfliche Sommerschloß Veitshöchheim, Zuflucht während der schwülheißen Zeit im Würzburger Kessel.

Ancient copper beech trees stand guard around the Prince-Bishops' summer palace in Veitshöchheim – a refuge from Würzburg's sweltering heat.

Des hêtres pourpre séculaires montent la garde autour du château d'été des princes-évêques qui fuyaient à Veitshöchheim la lourdeur moite des étés würzbourgeois.

Um der schwülen Hitze des Würzburger Kessels zu entgehen und leger zu leben, zogen sich die Fürstbischöfe im Sommer nach Veitshöchheim zurück. Schon 1683 war ein „Sommerhaus" nach Petrinis Plänen errichtet worden, dem Balthasar Neumann nach 1748 die Seitenpavillons anfügte. Die Umgestaltung des Zier- und Nutzgartens in eine prächtige Anlage im französischen Gartenstil erfolgte unter Adam Friedrich von Seinsheim. Ihm verdankt der Besucher die schnurgeraden Alleen, die gestutzten Hecken, vor allem das Wasserparterre und die zahlreichen Figuren aus dem heiteren Rokoko.

Im Nordosteck des Parks steht das Schlößchen auf einer quadratischen Terrasse, deren Felder Teppichgärtnereien tragen. Auf der westlichen und südlichen Mauer stehen elf weibliche und zwei männliche Steinfiguren, von Wolfgang van der Auwera geschaffen, die man als die neun Musen mit Apoll und Hermes, Minerva und Venus gedeutet hat. Aus der Auwera-Werkstatt stammen auch die beiden kräftigen Schweizer, die am Tor die Auffahrt zum Schlößchen bewachen.

Vier große Hauptgänge, die von Nord nach Süd ziehen, zerlegen den Garten in Zonen („Quartiere"). Den westlichsten begrenzen

Zahlreiche Göttinnen und Götter erinnern im Veitshöchheimer Schloßpark an eine entschwundene Welt. Künstliche Ruinen antiker Tempel säumen den Weg zum Schneckenhäuschen.

Dozens of gods and goddesses in the Veitshöchheim palace park remind us of a lost world. Artificial temple ruins styled after classical antiquity line the path to the Schneckenhäuschen (Snail House).

Déesses et dieux en grand nombre dans le parc du château de Veitshöchheim nous rappellent un temps suranné. Des ruines artificielles de temples antiques bordent le chemin menant à la petite maison aux coquillages: «Schneckenhäuschen».

Wände von Hainbuchen, die Hauptallee hat niedrige Korneliuskirschenhecken, von beschnittenen Linden überschattet. Der dritte Gang besitzt, was ganz ungewöhnlich für den Barock war, eine Fichtenallee, die übernommen wurde; der östliche Gang wird von Hainbuchenwänden begleitet. Die Stirnseiten sind als Aussichtspunkte herausgehoben. So führt die Hauptallee auf ein Gitter zu, das einmal einen Blick in die Landschaft freigab, endet der mittlere Quergang an der Kaskade, einem prächtigen Schaustück.

Charakteristisch für diesen Schloßpark ist der Große See mit seinen ein- und ausschwingenden Ufern mit den mächtigen Trauerweiden, die erst 1825, wie die Platanen am Kleinen See nebenan, auf Geheiß des Kronprinzen Ludwig gepflanzt wurden. Seepferd und Seewidder verspritzen Wasser vor dem Felsen inmitten des Sees, an dessen Flanken Apoll mit den Musen sich lagert, auf dessen Gipfel Pegasus, einst vergoldet, sich aufbäumt. Ferdinand Dietz, den der Fürstbischof von seinem Schloß Seehof bei Bamberg abzog, schuf die Figurengruppe. In den Nischen der Heckenwände, die den Weg um den See begleiten, stehen Figuren, die sich auf die vier Jahreszeiten beziehen.

Das Rondell inmitten der zweiten Zone ist von den Figuren der vier Erdteile und Tänzerpaaren umstellt. Von dort führen Gänge zu kleinen Plätzen und von dort diagonal zu luftigen Gartenhäusern, deren Decken zart bemalt sind. In dieser Heckenregion verbringen die Putten, als Kavaliere und Damen des Hofes kostümiert, ihr Leben mit Musik und Maskerade.

Das „Schneckenhäusle“, eine Grotte mit aufgesetztem Belvedere, ist das Entzücken der Kinder, weil die auf den Stuck gedrückten Glasflüsse und farbigen Steinchen wunderbar schimmern und die ganz aus Muscheln gebildeten Tiere den Betrachter beäugen.

Durch- und Ausblicke entlang der Heckenwände überraschen beim gemächlichen Spaziergang durch den Veitshöchheimer Hofgarten. Ruhebänke in den Pavillons laden zum gemütlichen Verweilen ein.

Views along and through the hedged wall of the Hofgarten in Veitshöchheim surprise the casual stroller. Park benches in the pavilions provide the ideal setting for a moment of contemplation and relaxation.

Des bancs invitent au repos et à la contemplation lors d'une promenade, toujours renouvelée, dans le parc du château de Veitshöchheim où constamment, entre les murs de haies, s'ouvrent des enfilades, des vues panoramiques qui nous surprennent et nous charment.

Veitshöchheim

Pleasure Palace of the Past

In order to get out of Würzburg's stifling heat, the Prince-Bishops used to retreat to Veitshöchheim during the leisurely summer months. There was a "summer house" there as early as 1683 and in 1748 Balthasar Neumann added on the side pavilions. Adam Friedrich von Seinsheim was called in to tranform the flower and vegetable gardens into a marvelous pleasure park in the best French style. He was responsible for the rows of walks, the neatly trimmed hedges and especially for the addition of the ponds and the numerous playful statues that are so typically Rococo. The summer palace, situated in the northeast corner of the park, is perched upon a rectangular terrace which is decorated with squares of grass and flowers. Wolfgang van der Auwera sculptured the eleven female and two male figures which adorn the south and west terrace walls. They represent the nine Muses plus Apollo and Hermes and Minerva and Venus.
Unlike their French prototype, the palace gardens in Veitshöchheim extend mainly in one direction, off to the west. Thus the palace in no longer the focal point of activity, no longer the absolute center of attention. The Franconian Prince-Bishops demonstrated that they had a mind of their own in that the reception path leading from the village to the palace remained relatively short, almost less representative in style than many of the other paths throughout the gardens. The two corpulent Swiss guards at the entrance gate are from Auwera's workshop.

Four main paths running in a north-south direction divide the park into "zones" or "quarters". Walls of hornbeam adorn the two outer pathways while lime trees towering over low decorative cherry hedges line the main pathway. The fourth path is somewhat unique for the Baroque – an already existing row of pines was incorporated into the overall design of the park. Viewpoints are cleverly located throughout the park; for example, the main walkway leads to a gate that once offered a view of the sprawling countryside; or, a crosspath leads to a lovely decorative cascade. The palace park is perhaps best known for its large pond whose perimeter curves in and out and which is surrounded by majestic weeping willows that were first planted in 1825 along with the plane trees around the small pond. Water spouts forth from sea horses and mythological rams around the mighty rock in the center of the pond where Apollo and the Muses are reclining. Pegasus rears at the top. The fountain was originally in white porcellan and gold. The statues in the hedged niches that ornament the path around the pond represent the four seasons. Statues of children depicting architecture and sculpture, painting and astronomy set off the arbors. The rondel in the second "quarter" is surrounded by dancing pairs and statues representing four of the continents. Narrower paths jet out diagonally to shady garden houses with delicately painted ceilings. Putti figures dressed as cavaliers and ladies-in-waiting lead a life of music and masquerade as they reign among the hedges while among the trees mythical moral figures found their place after the badly-damaged statues from the Italian comedy were removed in 1791. These figures never seem isolated or out of place, instead, they are an integral part of the park and its landscape. Peter Wagner's Apollo, who was moved here to the park wall, is the exception. Wagner also sculptured Bacchus and Venus in front of the grotto house.
This "Snail House", a grotto topped with a belvedere, always manages to delight young and old alike with its mosaics of colorful stones and bits of glass that glitter in the sunlight. The lions, monkeys and dragons made out of thousands of seashells throw quizzical glances at their onlookers. These animals demonstrate just how far the Rococo allowed its joviality and playfulness to be carried. The "Chinese" houses are a whim of the times: they are constucted atop massive stone tables upon which frugal meals were served. The servants sat with their backs to their masters and cooled the wine in the springs nearby.

Veitshöchheim

Château de plaisance d'autrefois

Pour fuir la chaleur et la moiteur de Würzburg trop encaissé entre les rives du Main, les princes-évêques quittaient la ville en été et se retiraient à Veitshöchheim où ils trouvaient fraîcheur et vie moins étouffante. Dès 1685 une résidence d'été y avait été construite d'après les plans de Petrini; Balthasar Neumann y ajouta une aile en 1748. Mais c'est à Adam Friedrich von Seinsheim que nous devons la magnificence du jardin à la française remplaçant les anciens jardins et potagers, avec ses allées rectilignes s'entrecoupant, ses haies taillées au cordeau et, avant tout, la pièce d'eau et les nombreuses statues qui nous introduisent dans les plaisirs de l'époque baroque.

Le petit château, au nord-est du parc, est construit sur une terrasse carrée dont le décor floral est un tapis. Sur les murs, à l'ouest et au sud, on remarque treize statues de pierre de Wolfgang van der Auvera: les neuf muses avec Apollon et Hermes puis Minerve et Vénus. Les deux Suisses robustes qui montent la garde au portail proviennent aussi de l'atelier de Auvera.

Quatre grandes allées partant du nord vers le sud divisent le jardin. A l'ouest de hautes haies de hêtres, des bosquets ombragés de tilleuls taillés au centre, et même, ce qui est tout à fait inhabituel à l'époque baroque, une allée de pins alors qu'à l'est on retrouve les hauts murs de hêtres. Le jardin est conçu pour permettre des vues panoramiques; c'est ainsi que l'allée centrale mène à une grille ouvragée qui donnait autrefois sur un paysage bucolique. La voie transversale, elle, donne sur la magnifique pièce d'eau. Ce parc est en effet caractérisé par le grand étang aux rives galbées, aux somptueux saules pleureurs plantés, ainsi que les platanes du petit bassin adjacent, en 1825, sur l'ordre du dauphin Louis. Chevaux et béliers marins font jaillir l'eau du roc central sur les flancs duquel Apollon et ses muses s'ébattent tandis qu'au sommet Pégase, autrefois doré, rue magnifiquement. Cet ensemble de statues, à l'origine dorées et blanches comme la porcelaine dont on venait de découvrir la fabrication en Europe, sont l'œuvre de Ferdinand Dietz que le prince-évêque fit venir exprès de son château de Seehof, près de Bamberg. Dans les niches des bosquets entourant le lac, des statues se rapportent aux quatre saisons, alors que, dans les charmilles, des groupes d'enfants représentent l'architecture, les arts plastiques, la peinture et l'astronomie.

La pelouse ronde au centre de la seconde zone est entourée de statues représentant les quatre continents et des couples de danseurs et de danseuses. De là partent des couloirs menant à de plus petites places et ensuite, diagonalement, d'autres encore vont vers de légers kiosques dont les plafonds sont peints de couleurs pastel. Si dans ce coin de bosquets les petits amours baroques costumés en dames et chevaliers servants passent agréablement leur temps à danser et se costumer, on trouve dans la région plus sylvestre les représentations des morales des fables de La Fontaine. Elles remplacent les figures de la comédie italienne ornant le théâtre en plein air qui en furent chassées dès 1791, à l'exception de l'Apollon sculpté par Peter Wagner que l'on voit repoussé contre le mur du jardin. C'est aussi à Peter Wagner que nous devons Bacchus et Vénus devant la grotte.

Cette petite maison de coquillages, «Schneckenhäusle», une grotte surmontée d'un belvédère, ravit les enfants, fascinés par les pierres de couleurs et de verre appliquées dans le stuc de la façade et les animaux entièrement formés de coquillages qui regardent le passant. Un divertissement à la mode de ce temps-là, comme les «Pavillons chinois» que Tietz fit construire au-dessus de lourdes tables de pierre sur lequelles on servait un repas frugal.